YOGA
for
Young India

YOGA
for
Young India

YOGA GURU OMO

Vitasta
Let Knowledge Spread

Published by
Vitasta Publishing Pvt. Ltd.
2/15, Ansari Road, Daryaganj,
New Delhi - 110 002
info@vitastapublishing.com

ISBN 978-93-80828-97-8

First Edition 2013
Third Reprint 2022
MRP ₹ 395

The views and opinions expressed in this book are the author's own. He is solely responsible for the facts and authenticity of the quotes and sources used for this work. The publisher is in no way liable for the same.

Cover & Layout Design by Vitasta Publishing Pvt. Ltd.
Printed by Vits Press, New Delhi

This book is dedicated to
children of the entire world

Contents

Preface

Patanjali's *Yoga Sutram* is a very important treatise. It explains Yoga very simply and in few words, explaining how to realize your own Self and how to live in a society with honour and dignity.

Patanjali was a practitioner of Indian medicine, a Siddha, and a commentator who is believed to have lived about 150 to 200 years before Christ, somewhere in western Tamilnadu of today. He is said to have first evolved a set of dance movements, and then he perfected what we know as yoga postures.

Although yoga was developed and practiced thousands of years ago, it is relevant even now, in the 21st century. It is often said that yoga and meditation heal an individual bodily, mentally, and spiritually. Most people are confused because of so many, so called 'definitions' and interpretations of yoga.

This book attempts to clear the misconceptions and misunderstandings about yoga and meditation. It tries to help young people understand, first the philosophy behind a healthy body and a healthy mind, and then the practice.

Yoga means realization of the ultimate reality, which is said to be the realization of Self. Once a person understands one's own self, one understands the higher being, which is the spiritual reality. To realize the ultimate reality, there is a process, a way.

Unionization, or becoming one with the divine, is yoga but the way for realization is also called yoga.

Maharshi Patanjali has specified the 'eight limbs of yoga', which are called the Astangyoga (1) Yam (2) Niyam (3) Asan (4) Pranayam (5) Pratyahar (6) Dharna (7) Dhyan and lastly (8) Samadhi.

It is necessary to know about all the eight limbs of yoga, in brief.

Patanjali clarifies how to live in society ethically, following the Yam and how to realize God following Niyam.

Patanjali has given us this treatise for perpetual peace and harmony. The process starts at an individual level. Which types of persons are essential for society? How can they be moulded? Patanjali emphasises Yamas for social or collective upliftment and Niyamas for the personal or individual upliftment. Yamas and Niyamas are the ultimate ways to keep individuals and society in order. So these are very strong tools for yoga. Yoga is yoga due to these Yamas and Niyamas. Thus, Yoga is a way and also the ultimate realization.

Yam consists of five practices/terms:

I. Ahimsa (nonviolence)

II. Satya (truthfullness)

III. Asteya (no stealing)

IV. Aparigraha (no hoarding)

V. Brahmacharya (celibacy)

Ahimsa-non violence, means not to hurt anyone mentally, verbally or physically. Satya means to stay on the path of truth. Asteya means not to steal anything from anyone. Aparigraha means not to have things more than your needs. Brahmacharya means to observe celibacy.

Niyam consists of five practices/terms:

I. Sauch (Sanctity)

II. Santosh (Contentment)

III. Tapa (Austerity)

IV. Swadhyay (Study of holy scriptures)

V. Ishwar-pranidhan (Surrender to God)

Sauch means cleanliness, Santosh means contentment, a satisfactory approach, Tapa means austerity, to have the stamina for suffering the contra and critical situations. Swadhyay means study of the scriptures to acquire a rationalized perspective and Ishwarpranidhan means surrender to God.

So, Yamas and Niyamas set the terms and conditions for yoga practitioners. These lay the moral foundation for not only yoga practitioners but also for every person to become a great citizen of the world. They are similar to the Ten Commandments that Moses handed down to his people.

Here I am not going to tell you in detail about the third and fourth limbs of Astangyoga, Asan and Pranayam because a thorough introduction to them has been given in the fourth and fifth chapters of this book. Yes, Pratyahar means to withdraw the senses from the respective subjects.

Dharana, Dhyan and Samadhi are described elaborately in the chapter on meditation.

The book is full of knowledge of the hermits of the Himalayas and is ready to introduce briefly this heritage of India's sages to the world.

The purpose of writing this book is to impart this great inherited knowledge to our children in a very logical and scientific manner because today's world is defined in the terminology of science. Without scientific approach and experiments, no one likes to accept even fact as fact. So this book is deliberately formated on the basis of experiments because yoga is one perspective of science. Yoga is getting popular all over the world because of its scientific and therapeutic base. Yoga is a science and it must be taught as a science to all children.

This book is not only for kids aged five to six, but also for young adults because all of us are kids before Rishis and Munies, sages and hermits, monks and Babas, Saints and Mahatmas. Everyone is a child unless God is realized. Every child can be more efficient than he or she is, through practice of yoga and meditation. This book is a result of years of research and it is hoped, it will prove useful not only for children and young adults but also for every beginner, hesistantly approaching the world of yoga.

Yoga practices protects all parts and organs of the body, while gym exercises concentrate on only muscle building. The benefits which are expected from a gym are available through yoga practice also. Yoga cares for the all-round development of the body and the mind.

— Yoga Guru Omo

One

Yoga Tradition and Trends

Meaning and Motif

The answer to the question 'What is Yoga?' requires authenticity. This answer, therefore, needs to come from none other than Maharashi Patanjali, the great sage of yoga. His book about yoga is *Yoga Sutram*, which is considered a classic. This is the most authentic book of yoga. Maharashi Patanjali answers the question with an aphorism [अथयोगानुशासनम् (Athayoganushasanam)] "yoga is discipline or discipline is yoga". This is the exact answer for the question, 'what is yoga?'

Yoga existed before Patanjali too. From the Rigvedic era, yoga was in vogue. Maharshi Patanjali had to cover a vast ground to further the yogic knowledge systematically. This yoga, however, was not in formulation but individually dispersed experiences at the time of the Maharshi. Patanjali took the best out of the then existing practices, aphorized (made concise) and made it apprehensive as a textual treatise for all of us.

Patanjali perused all the views and ideas concerning yoga, and only then did he revolutionize the traditional concepts and ideas of yoga. Yoga is tradition and Patanjali was not the first to modify it and systemise it. Maharshi Kapil was another sage who was known to have forwarded the knowledge of yoga for coming generations. Each and every sage knew well about yoga, as a personal persuite. Later, Maharshi Patanjali enriched and systematized it for those who are not sages.

There were some root words in Patanjali's mind. Those root words directed him to put the word 'discipline' in the aphorism.

First: *Yuj samadhau* means to attain the trance state of mind or the highest consciousnes.

Second: *Yugir yoge* means to unify.

Third: *Yuj Samayamane* means to temperate, to maintain the discipline in every way.

The word yoga originated from all the above three roots; and does not violate the meaning and spirit of the roots. Patanjali uses the word *Anushasanam* 'discipline' because the word discipline completely ratifies the traditional approach and justifies the spirit of yogic succession. So, Patanjali uses this particular word and states that 'yoga is discipline and discipline is yoga'.

The cosmos moves in a very disciplined way. All the milkyways move in a very disciplined manner. The whole solar family moves in a very disciplined way. All the planets move in their disciplined ways. If any planet of the solar family violates the discipline, a big bang may occur and a big hazard may take place. It is discipline which keeps the whole universe in order. It is discipline which makes a man great. It is discipline which makes society, the country and the nation great.

The whole universe rests on law and order. Nature is governed by its laws. All the nations are governed by laws. The object of Constitutions is only to maintain law and order, which means discipline. There is no violation of discipline in the whole universe, and if there is any violation, that's only among human beings. There is no violation among animals. Only human beings are indisciplined creatures because man is a social animal. So he violates the values and decorum of society, breaks rules and regulations, laws and orders of the society. Human beings disobey law and order.

The ultimate aim of yoga is to realize God and it is the human being who has this privilege. Therefore, the human being requires discipline and this discipline is nothing but yoga.

Yoga is, however, not for all the beings because all the beings have a limited capacity. Human being has unlimited capacity. Some human beings are rational, and some are rascals; human beings have efficacy or scope of rationality and rascality in a maximum way. Yoga is the science to ratify the rationality in human beings and to minimize the rascality in order to tune the human being to the order of nature or cosmos. The climax of the attunement is realization of the supreme entity or God.

Actually, this is yoga. Thus, discipline is a very important part of the creation.

Children are taught yoga in order to make them disciplined and civilized, so that human beings can achieve the consequences of discipline or the fruits of discipline. Though there are many definitions of yoga, irrespective of this wideness of definition, that 'yoga is discipline and discipline is yoga' is seminalised. It is a base for all the definitions.

Yoga and Mindstuff

Patanjali uses a second aphorism to answer the question 'What is Yoga?' [योगश्चित्तवृत्तिनिरोधः (Yogashchittabritti nirodhaha)]. Yogah = Yoga, *Chitta* (mindstuff), Vrittih (thought waves), Nirodhah (containment). This means–the secession of thought waves in the mind. This is yoga.

This aphorism is the next step to the first. The first aphorism *Athayoganushasanam* means yoga is discipline and this second aphorism sets out the terms and conditions for its ultimate realization.

This is a scientific process to purify the mindstuff, to prepare the ground for realization and that is not possible without a disciplined approach in the daily routine of life.

Discipline is the ground and on that ground, the scientific process or technique is to be practised to stop thought waves or to delete thought waves from the mind or *Chitta* for realization of the Supreme being, the source of all the sources.

All efforts, whether these are at a personal level, social level, national level or global level, require discipline and order everywhere. Therefore, the composite meaning of the two aphorisms is: yoga is discipline and practise, for purification of *Chitta* or the mindstuff to realize the Supreme entity. This concept is accepted almost unanimously in every sect and philosophical tradition of India. There is a little difference in yogic and Vedantic concepts, but there is no great difference actually, which is clear from the figures given below:

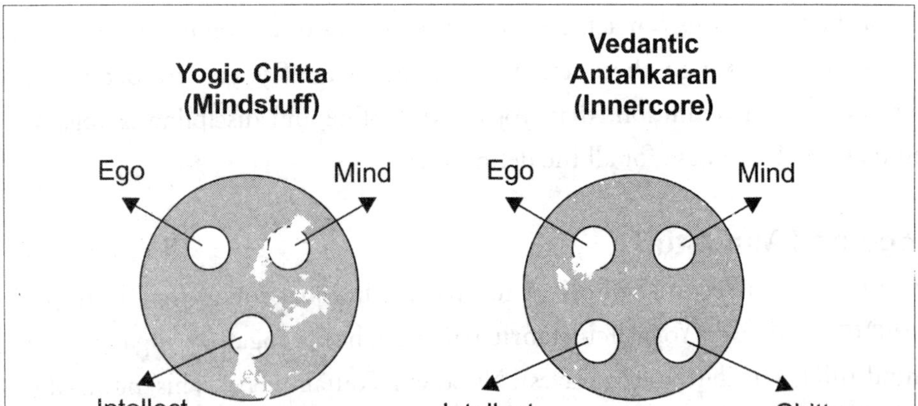

According to yogic concepts, the mind, intellect and ego are contained in *Chitta* and in the Vedanta, mind, intellect, ego and *Chitta* are composed in *Antahkaran* (the inner core). No difference at all. Only the style of presentation is different, but the letter and spirit of the two schools of thought are same.

This *Chitta* or mindstuff is the source of our mindset, life format, line of thinking, line of action, fate, luck, tendencies, dispositions, inclinations, nature and everything else. This mindstuff is covered with five layers of desires. This is especially true of the matrix, which is layered by specific characterstics of desire, which compels a person to don the mantle of a human being. Through meditation, all the dirty layers are to be deleted one by one. When all the layers of desire are deleted, then the *Chitta* becomes pure and yoga, or unity with divinity, takes place.

All the five layers are characterized by special symptoms and reflect the attitudes of a person. As the *Chitta* is purified, the symptoms also get changed and are reflected in the changed behavior of the person/meditator/practitioner. **(1) Mudh, (2) Kshipt (3) Vikshipt (4) Ekagra (5) Nirudh**

1. Mudh

This is the first layer of *Chitta* that reflects the nature and conduct of a person. Such a person has no civic sense. He acts like an idiot. The behaviour of such

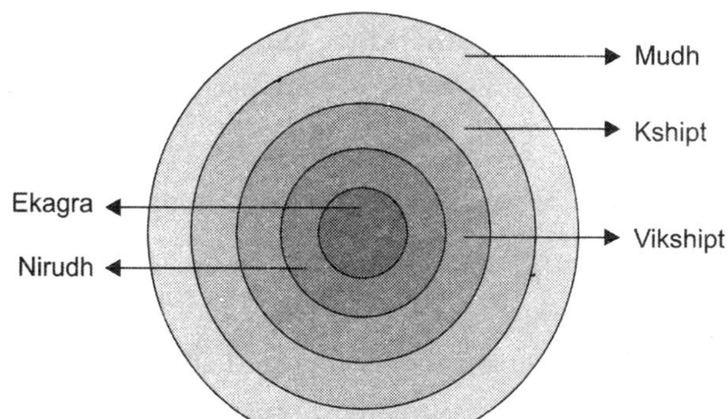

a person is very like an animal. He has no sense of cleanliness. The person is totally indisciplined and insensitive.

The tendency and behaviour of such a person is like an animal because, although he has the body of a human being, his psyche has not developed enough to be of human standard.

2. Kshipt

The reflection of this layer is better than that of Mudh. In this state, a person is better in tendency, behavior and conduct. The person is very selfish, a rascal and a cheater. The person is committed to his/her vested interests all the time, without any hesitation and guilty feeling. The person acts or campaigns for the gross interst of his/her sensual demands and needs. The characteristics of such a person are not good at all. The person is so clever and tricky, that he/she is an open cheater. They are gross egotists and envious of other competent and reputed persons. They always criticize famous and appreciable persons. They abuse wealthy persons, politicians and celebrities.

The psyche is self-centred in such people.

3. Vikshipt

In this state, the psyche of the person is full of benevolence.

Such a person thinks always of the wellfare of others. The person is pure-hearted. The person thinks for others first, and is a very philanthropic one. They are always busy with charity. They are very active. They always do something or the other. They like to be active always. They are very good activists in charity works. In society, they are considered very good people.

4. Ekagra

In this state of psyche, a person is very focussed and studious.

Such people are geniuses, thinkers, orators, writers and mental workers.

Such people are men of composure, men of austerity and men of ascetic life. Such people like to live alone. Such persons are meditators. The mind of such a person is very concentrated and is quite quiet.Their mind is very sharp and in such a state, a person becomes very pure- hearted and is always busy, always engaged. This state of the psyche is acquired as a result of cleansing of the three preceding layers of *Chitta.*

5. Nirudh

In such a state, the *Chitta* is clean or purified completely.

As it's name is Nirudh, it means no thought waves. This state is called the state of Yoga in the scriptures. This is the state where the realization takes place.

To acquire such a state, a retreat for yoga and meditation is required.

Without discipline nothing is achieved. All the spiritual practices and meditation retreats require discipline. So discipline is yoga.

The purified state of the mind is yoga, and it is possible only then, when all thought waves are quietend. There must not be any waves (ripples of thought) in the mindstuff or *Chitta.* This state, according to Patanjali, is yoga.

This is an authentic answer to the question 'what is yoga?' In this manner, the ground definition, 'yoga is discipline and discipline is yoga', holds true. On this ground of discipline, the process for any meditative technique can be practised. Then alone can the process of purification of the mindstuff get a chance and the culmination of the practice of yoga is fructified.

The way of practice may be different but discipline is required everywhere, in every path of spirituality; in every religious format of worship discipline is a must. All methods of worship require discipline and patience. So, it is the universal and bed-rocky definition and meaning of yoga.

Maharshi Patanjali was very sagacious, very sharp minded, farsighted and transcendental. So he formulated a 'total philosophy' of yoga, which was scattered over the entire Vedic era and gave us an explicit foundation and formulation of yoga, so that we may not misconceive or be misguided in the name of yoga.

Most of the definitions of yoga are inherited from this basic yoga aphorisms by Maharshi Patanjali. No definition can ignore this ground definition and if ignored, then that will be base-less.

This is a scanning definition. Wherever and whenever you find any dialogue and debate on what is yoga, scan always through this definition that yoga is discipline and discipline is yoga.

Maharshi Patanjali answers the question 'what is yoga?' in his *Yoga Sutram's* first aphorism–that yoga is discipline–but after this staunch statement on discipline, what is one to do or what is the purpose of this staunch disciplic ground?

If there is a discipline, then there must be a purpose. Otherwise, what is the use of such a discipline? Maharshi Patanjali says clearly (Yogaschittavrittinirodhah) yoga is nothing but the purification of the *Chitta*, mindstuff or the cessation of thought waves in the mind. When the mind is purified, this state is known *Brahmisthiti* or the state of trance. This is a premature state of mind, where the scope of intuition and clairvoyance is attained and all the divine virtues rain over the practitioner.

The cessation of thought waves is not possible without the disciplic ground. So, Maharshi Patanjali has imparted the foundation that is all- pervasive and all-inclusive, but here, this definition is for the spiritual practitioners. Without pure heart or the purification of *Chitta*, there is no scope for upliftment in yogic exercises and practice of meditation. The climax of yoga is not achieved.

The process of purification of mindstuff is done only in the state of discipline.

The purification of mindstuff is like deletion of matter from the hard disc of a computer or CD. The storage of many past births, imprints and wills, are the matrix of our thinking and doing. The *Chitta* is where pain and pleasure is experienced. Our present life is a tiny manifestation of our unlimited wills and actions, bad and good.

Through meditation, all the matters are burnt from the soft disc or the

Chitta. All pleasure and pain are deleted or burnt one by one. In this way, the practitioner deletes all the causes of the circle of death and birth. Therefore, the science of meditation is a mere way to get rid of all the queries, compulsions and at last, the Yogi attains yoga through skill or expertise and assiduous retreat to the state of meditation.

Just as God is One, in the same way, the Yoga is One. The ways are many–worship, prayer, Namaz, Kirtan, Japa, Tapa, Bhajan, meditation etc. The ways may be different, but the character of all the ways cannot be very different. The culmination of all the ways is only one, the mercy of God, in joining the kingdom of God and the unionization with the Supreme. This is super consciousness, Krishna consciousness, Jain consiousness, Buddha consciousness, Guru Nanak consciousness, Kabir and Sufi consciousness, Christ consiousness, and cosmic consciousness.

Yoga Skill and Equanimity

The *Shrimad Bhagavatgita* has some very popular statements which are generally quoted during common conversations:[(Samatumyoga-muchyate) (समत्वं योग उच्यते)] and [(Yoga karmssu kausalam). (योग: कर्मस्सु कौशलम्).]

Both these sayings do not violate the letter and spirit of aphorism of the *Yoga Sutram*, thereby denoting that yoga is discipline and discipline is yoga.

Lord Krishna says, 'Rest in yoga and work in the spirit of detachment, be poised, in success or failure'. This is the state of yoga or this is the 'Yoga'.

This state means–evenness is the ground for realization or unionization of self into a cosmic existence, the mergence of the individual intelligence into ultimate intelligence. The communion of the mind into the spirit. This is achievable through meditation.

The *Gita* is the scripture of the art of proper action, so that everyone may learn it and elevate himself/herself to the spiritual height. This art of action requires learning and practice. Learning and practice requires regularity and discipline.

In the temporal world, every learning or any skill or expertise requires special terms and conditions. In the same way, the spiritual world also requires terms and condition to get ahead towards perfection.

Everywhere, in every aspect of life of a human being, expertness or skill is a must and if skill is a must, then discipline is also a must because without discipline, expertise is not achievable and without skill any achievement is not possible.

Every profession requires expertise, not clumsiness. A clumsy person can do nothing in any field, not to speak of perfection. For any job or service, special trainings and courses are arranged everywhere. During the course period and study, staunch discipline is a must. Then, and then only, does the training makes the trainees fit or professional.

In God realization also, specific training is compulsory for a specific person, and that is the science of meditation. The hi-techniques of meditation and premeditation is a scientific process.

Just as everyone requires an expert teacher to learn any skill in any field, in the same way, spiritual life also expects an expert teacher of yoga and meditation. So the *Guru* is a crucial need for 'promotion' and 'perfection', in the life of human beings, whether material or spiritual. In this way, it is the disciplic practice that makes man perfect.

This is why Maharshi Patanjali provides an all-expanded meaning of yoga as a 'seed' in his scripture of yoga.

He says, only a disciplined person can give lessons of discipline to the beginers, and then the disciplic succession goes on for generations and this is the yoga tradition, the handing-over of knowledge to the next generation, for the continuation of this great and grand tradition.

Now a days, the word 'yoga' is very popular everywhere, especially in the western world. The word conjures up the image of huts and the heritage of the hermits of the Himalayas of India. It is their contribution to the world. Millions of people from the west come to India to learn the science of yoga and meditation. In a broad way, yoga means the unionization of self into the cosmic, or the merging of the mind into cosmic intelligence. This is the ultimate state of yoga but few practice the correct way to achieve this ultimate state called yoga.

Most people think that yoga means some physical exercises, some postures, some gymnastic gestures, some jumping and jogging, and walking, some quick or deep breathings and so on. They do not know that those physical exercises or postures pertain to just one wing of yoga. That in Yama, Niyam, Asana, Pranayam, Pratyahar, Dharana, Dhyana and *Samadhi*, all the exercises are nothing but *Asanas*. That asanas are only postures, not yoga. This is only part of the process to reach the state of 'yoga' or union with the supreme being. This is the way to realization or yoga. Appreciatively, people call the process also as yoga.

Yoga is actually an ultimate stage, unity with divinity, but all the means and ways also are addressed as yoga. Maharshi Patanjali states that *Astangayoga* means the eight-fold path of yoga, which is a systematic and scientific way to reach towards trance or *Samadhi*.

The *Samadhi* is the climax of the process or the way.

So the ways, the processes are also called yoga. The concept is superfluous because it means only a very hard regime of physical exercises, to achieve fitness of physique alone. Some people project themselves as great yogis, based just on their abilities to exercise. People generally respect such fitness experts a great deal.

The physical exercises maintain the discipline of the inner metabolic function and activity of the endocrine glands. For this purpose, just some specific exercises are sufficient. Only to practices the asanas or postures is not real yoga. One must keep this in mind, then alone can the meaning and motif of yoga be properly understood.

Offshoots of Yoga

Many terms are in vogue in the name of yoga. Often, the beginner is confused by the names: ***Kriya-yoga, Bhaktiyoga, Karmyoga, Hathayoga,*** **Jnanyoga,**

Dhyanyoga, *Asthangyoga,* Rajyoga, Mantrayoga, *Tantrayoga, Kundaliniyoga, Power yoga* and so on.

It is remarkable that every word is linked to yoga. Without the word 'yoga', none of the names would mean anything, because all the words are the processes or ways towards yoga. They are methods to unionize with the soul. Here too, Patanjali provides the solution, with an aphorism. He clarifies the founding secret of his predecessors in this definition तपः स्वाध्यायेश्वर प्रणिधानानि क्रियायोगः Tapah = austerity, swadhyay= scriptural study related to yoga and spirituality, Ishwar Pranidhanani = Surrender to the will of God. This means, ***Kriyayoga*** is nothing but the composition of austerity, scriptural study and surrender to God.

This definition covers all the definitions given above.

If any person is very lazy, non-punctual and has no austerity in his life, then how can he be a yogi? This is the first term and condition of ***Kriya-yoga.***

The second term and condition is scriptural perusal or study, because any person may be very austere but may not know the object of yoga. The concept is not clear to him, nor does he know about yoga. The person who does not fulfill this term and condition can never succeed.

The third condition is surrender to God, trust in truth, trust in the super will, the submission in the will of God, full devotion to the lotus feet of the Supreme Being. All the three conditions are the summum bonum of yoga. Yoga is nothing but the composition of austerity, rationality and devotionality. These are the three pillars on which the dome of yoga rests.

If any pillar is weak or fragile, the dome gets imbalanced and collapses. Here, through austerity, the body is being disciplined. Through rationality, intellect is being disciplined and through devotion, the mind is being disciplined. The three conditions maintain discipline in one's daily routine.

The whole of yoga is called ***Bhaktiyoga.*** Devotion is emphasized here, because being austere and rational, if there is no faith or reverence or love for God, both are useless. In the same way if there is only devotion and no understanding, then fundamentalism surfaces. Without rationality, intolerance erupts. Therefore, a proportionate ratio in the three conditions is compulsory. No definition crosses the frame of this three-pillared definition of Maharshi Patanjali.

Why is the word *Karmayoga* used? *Karmayoga* is yoga through karma or work. It means to serve God, to please God, serving all the beings. For work, austerity, sagacity, sentiments and commitments are a must. Here too, there is a basis of three conditions, only then is it *Karmayoga*.

Karmayoga means duty for the sake of duty. To work in the spirit of loving and serving God, to see God in every being, to act or pass life in the service of all such beings is *Karmayoga*, a selfless service.

Why is the ***Hathayoga*** word used for yoga? 'Hath' or 'hata' is a Sanskrit word which means obstinacy. Actually, no one takes to spirituality easily, and one has to force one's self to engage with divinity.

'Ha + Tha=Hath. Ha means *Ingla* and Tha means *Pingla*. These are the nadis. The *Ingla* and *Pingla* nadis meet at the cerebrum or *Shasrar Chakra*. Yoga takes place and then the *Kundalini* wakes and goes through Susumna and realization happens. So it is called Hathyoga, it is similar to *Kundalini* yoga.

A hathayogi has to undergo the three conditions of austerity, rationality and devotion. No one wants austerity, everyone seeks leisure and pleasure, but when one gets convinced or rationalizes, then he or she gives up leisure and hugs yoga. So it is called Hathyoga, because that person engages himself forcibly in austerity. This definition also does not violates the spirit of Maharshi Patanjali's prominent definition, 'discipline is yoga and yoga is discipline'.

Why is the word ***Jnanyoga*** used for yoga? Because scriptural study is an important part of yoga. So, knowledge is focussed upon emphatically by some sections, in the quest for spirituality. If there is someone who gives more importance to the study of scriptures, his/her yoga is called *Jnanyoga*. Austerity, rationality and devotion helps realize the transcendental reality. The secret of the universe is unravelled and that is the *Jnan* or *Gyan*.

In Sanskrit, the word *Jnan* or '*Gyan*' is used for scriptural study as well as for the realization of the absolute reality, therefore, this state is known as Jnanayoga. This also does not violate the spirit of Patanjali's definition of Kriyayoga, because through the scriptural study, intellect, mind and ego, all get disciplined. The practitioner studies spiritual and moral texts always. He/she undergoes austerity and rationality. As soon as he/she advances his/her study, he/she realizes the magnitude of God and gradually surrenders to God. This is a way or the process of meditation and yoga.

Why is ***Dhyanyoga*** also used for this motif ? During *Sadhana*, Dhyan or meditation is done or practised, and then the supreme entity is realized. In this way, we find out that the realization is through the process of meditation. So it is called *Dhyanyoga*. The meaning of this term also comes within the letter and spirit of Maharshi Patanjali's aphorism because meditation requires austerity, discrimination of right and wrong and concrete trust in God. Then, and then only, is the secret of the universe revealed and that is called revelation.

All the terms are used aproximately, as most people who use these terms actually don't understand their specific meanings. Thus arises the debate about which is a superior practice. Therefore, Maharshi Patanjali has contained this superflous debate of superiority and inferiority among the various practices by coining one word, the ***Astangyoga***.

It is a very scientific way of maintaining discipline in a person. The formulation of such a scientific and systematic ground, to which the definition of Kriyayoga may be applied and fructified because all the terms are within the circle of the the aphorism of Kriyayoga, is the best way for realization or yoga.

Yam and Niyam are moral and ethical foundations for the practitioner. Asana and Pranayama are the physical relaxation, decarbonisation and oxygenation or to have a healthy, disease-free, purified body. Pratyahar is moderation and temperation of senses or discipline in sensual longing for subjects and objects. Dharna and Dhyan are the gradual concentration process in any form or symbol of God. This is the discipline of the mind and intellect, the overall purification of the mindstuff or *Chitta*. *Samadhi* is the climax of the scientific process of *Astangayoga* for the realization of the transcendental reality. This is a very disciplined process for yogic perfection.

Many missions, movements, and sects use the word *Rajyoga* like a patent. The word Raj means to brush or shine, or to lighten and illumine. Another meaning of this word is 'Raj' or kingly excellence. In the *Gita* it is appreciated well, that it is 'the king of knowledge, confidential, most sacred, most excellent, immediately effective, comfortable to practise. No harm in practising it'.

This is also a process to cleanse the mind and practise through meditative hi-tech exercises so that, at last, illumination is achieved by the practitioner. This ***Rajyoga*** also is not beyond the ambit of the three conditions–austerity, scriptural perusal and devotion to God. This is the way for discipline, and then the way of illumination or unionization of self with the divine or yoga is prepared.

Mantrayoga and ***Tantrayoga*** are also words used for yoga. Tantra means network or the points of power, mystic power. Our spinal cord has seven chakras, seven mystic points of power from the bottom of the spine up to the cerebrum. All the points have uncounted and charismatic capacities. Due to chanting of special mantra, the special Tantra, or the points of network of the special power/ chakras are awoken, and a special mystic potency or power is acquired by the practitioner. This is, therefore, called Mantra-Tantra-Yantrayoga.

Yantra is the instrument empowered by the Mantra, to activate the Tantras. The centre, or circle of power, is the talisman. Taabiz or the Ganda are the Tantras or the instruments for the power of the Mantra. Here too, austerity, rationality and devotion are the disciplic backgrounds. Through this mantra *sadhana*, many acquire mystic powers and can demonstrate it's power.

Many tantriks and magicians have such powers. Someone uses this power with bonafide intention and someone with malafide intention. This is now-a-days called the 'Mantra therapy'. It is a very risky method of meditation. If errors and omissions occur during the practice of this *sadhana*, it may result in very tragic consequences for the body and the mental mechanism. In this case, the practitioner practises yogic inputs of mantra, but forgets the omnipotent God. He makes efforts to aquire godly powers, to be powerful among fellow creatures and to bulldoze others. So, in a way, this person exposes himself to divine punishments. Such people suffer the bad side-effects of mantras.

It is only an impatient person who likes such a yoga. As far as the 'power' or potency of yoga is concerned, all the powers are acquired sequentially, through the bonafide, meditative retreat. Adi Guru Shankarcharya warned against tantra and mantra, said no to its practise due to the hazardous and tragic nature of the sufferings for practitioners who went wrong.

The purpose of *sadhana* is to attain liberation and not to gain power and violate cosmic rules. This is spiritual terrorism, a punitive act. This is also not out of any sense of discipline. No one violates the definition of Kriyayoga and its three terms and conditions. There are so many mantras. Specific mantras are for specific mystic powers, but there is a risk in incorrect chantings which damage the neural and mental mechanism.

Only the *Gayatri mantra* is said to be the greatest mantra for spiritual elevation, also for the protection of the body and for good health. To avoid sudden death, the Mahamritunjaya mantra is also very efficacious. These have no bad side effects. These are very positive mantras.

The *Gayatri mantra's* vibration, of continuous repetitive chanting, concentrates the spinal mystic points all together, and elevates the chanter spiritually. Though, after twelve years of continuous chanting, all the powers erupt, but by that time the practitioner actually never cares about his mystic achievements. The mantra's power acts like a password or code number that affects the targeted network or programming. So, full of compassion, Adi Shankaracharya warned us against this Tantra-Mantra yoga. Yes, if there is no nalafide motif, then there is no prohibition in its practice.

There are so many ways for unionization or yoga. There must be no confusion that yoga is a way and yoga is also an ultimate realization. One is the way, the other is the goal, one must not be confused for the other.

Kundaliniyoga is called *kundalini* yoga because the power and potency is curled in the muladhar chakra, which is the last power point of the spinal cord. This gets activated and then the realization happens. This is the climax of *sadhana* that happens through a scientific process.

Kundalini means a serpent, coiled energy dormant at the bottom of the spine. As soon as the Chitta or mindstuff gets empty of the vices and virtues, a vacuum is created. This accelerates a magnetic field in the cerebrum or Sahasrarchakra. This magnetic power attracts the coiling energy–'Kundalini'–and this *Kundalini* rises up to cover the vacuum in the cerebrum. And this is the moment of realization. This happening gives the meditator the capacity to be enlightened or achieve realization. So it is known as Kundaliniyoga.

Power Yoga the word power yoga is also in use these days. This is nothing but the same yoga exercises which give 'power'. It is, however, not necessary to use yoga especialy to gain 'power'.

The effect of all yogic postures and exercises is to empower the weak and fragile muscles and nervous system. Through the practice of some specific exercises, stamina and strength is aquired. Particular glands are activated which provides sexual stamina. It is, therefore, called power yoga. This word 'power', here, is used in a minor sexual sense, irrespective of the huge purpose of yoga. To woo exhausted persons, the word 'power' is very atractive. So it is used and advertised as a booster of sexual power, with advise to use some herbs too, for permanent sexual potency.

Thus, we see that there is different usage of the word yoga, most of the ways aim to attain the Supreme or 'Yoga', but not all are ways of divine illumination.

ॐ ॐ ॐ

Two

Basic Principles of Yoga

The basic principle of yoga is to maintain harmony in the entire cosmos. Harmony within the body, harmony within the family, harmony within the nation and harmony over the entire globe. The root unit of harmony is the individual and among people, children are the root unit and posess fresh minds for learning the science of harmony, love, life, peace and God.

The Rishis and Munis gave us the philosophy and practice of 'yoga' in order to ensure harmony in the whole human population. When a child is in harmony with the world, then whole of society and humanity is in harmony too. Yoga is the greatest and the best tool to creat this harmony among kids. Yoga is a complete, anxiety-and fear-preventive therapy for children.

Our ancient sages formulated some specific yogic postures and exercises, and they gave us tips for etiquette as well as punishment, to apply in our daily lives. This is to maintain and restore harmony in physiological and psychological levels. The physiological and psychological harmony prepare the ground for spiritual harmony, which is the purpose of every human life.

Yoga and Children

The great sages have prescribed yogic ways for parents and teachers to treat and behave with kids according to their age, predispositions and requirements for their well being.

They have prescribed systems and methods to develop a child's inherent potential and make a child into a complete, healthy, staunch and responsible person in society.

पंच वर्षाणि लालयेत द्वादश वर्षाणि ताडयेत ।
सम्प्राप्ते षोडश वर्षे तु पुत्रं मित्रं समाचरेत ।।

Panch varshani lalayet dwadash varshani tadayet.
Samprapte shodash varshe tu putram mitram samacharet.

The verse above is from the *Chanakyaneeti*. Chanakya's laws and rules of ethics tell us how to treat children. This verse clarifies how to treat children in childhood and how to treat a growing kid and an adolescence youth.

- The great Guru says that, a child, up to the age of five deserves only love. He/she must never be snubbed or threatened, never be beaten or ostracised. Parents must love children up to five years old very much.
- When the children reach six years of age, they must be taught to be disciplined. This lessons must continue up to age twelve. Between age 6-12 is the time to teach kids. At this age, a child may be punished–but only through some yogic practice and never in anger. Six to twelve years time duration is enough time to discipline a child.
- When children reach 16 years of age, then they must be treated as friends. Only friendship can protect the cordial relationships and brin harmony

in the family. This is the best formula, given by the great Guru, Chankya.

Chanakya tells us, 6-12 is the age for training kids as good or bad persons. So, the punishment must not be any form of physical or mental torture. It should only be more teaching, more lessons and training and instilling discipline among the kids, to make them used to good habits and attitudes, behaviour so essential for society, the country and the world.

Discipline is yoga and yoga is discipline, and this can make a child a good human being as an adult and a great person. Discipline is nothing but caution and awareness, always and everywhere, about the benefits and harms in life.

When a child is born, the Mother is the first and formost Guru (teacher). She teaches and treats the child *regularity* and *discipline* through disciplic nurturing. Mother moulds the child as a good and productive citizen of the world.

The sages prescribed prostration and genuflection for paying obeisance in the Gurukuls/boarding schools of the past, to bring under control naughty and mischievous children. The Rishis were well aware that if any child plays mischief, then the root cause is in the psyche not in the physique. If the psyche is vagarant and vibrant, it would reflect in the physique as an ill action, misbehaviour or bad, odd and awkward acts.

Yoga and Etiquette

Yoga practice makes a child very humble, polite, decent and good mannered. It also makes him/her efficient and confident. Yoga practice provides physical and mental stamina to children. Yoga and its practice is, thus, a boon for kids.

In India, for the expression of honour and respect to anyone, some specific ways are prescribed. All these ways are nothing but yogic postures, which are very effective in harmonizing the physique and the psyche because of their therapeutic nature. The four main ways of greeting, paying respect are:

I. Prostration/Sastang /Dandvat pranam

II. Jaanunaman/Genuflection

III. Charan Sparsh/Touching Feet
IV. Namastey or Namaskar/Salutation

Prostration/Dandvat/Sastang Pranam

This manner of salutation is in vogue even today in the spiritual world.

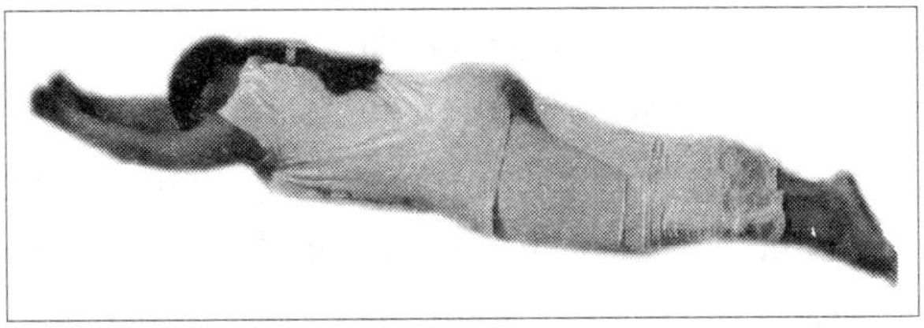

Among Sadhus and Mahatmas this way of expression is to pay respect to seniors, masters, Gurus and teachers. Dandvat Pranam, means to lie down on the belly and touch the forehead to the ground before the feet of the revered, flat like a straight stick.

It is an expression of complete surrender, full of reverence. In the temples before the idols of God, demigods and deities, devotees pay obeissance like wise. Pupils pay obeissance to their Gurus in this manner. Sastang pranam means salutation, using eight organs–the head, eyes, ears, nose, chest, belly, hands and feet–before the revered. So it is called eight-fold salutation or Sastang pranam.

Psycho-somatic benefits

1. In such posture, the whole body touches the ground and the forehead the earth. Palms of the hand are joined together and stretched. The gravitational force attracts all the blood vessels and blood atoms in such a posture. Half the portion of the body is brimming with blood and gives pressure to the head, heart, belly and genitalia, which revitalises children's physical capacities.
2. In such posture, the forehead touches the ground. Excess of electromagnetic waves in an overactive child is absorbed by the earth and the child relaxes.
3. Fullness and pressure in the head portion increases the ratio of blood in heart, neck, face, throat, eyes, nose, ears, brain, cheeks, tongue, etc. which energizes and makes all the organs more sensitive and active.

4. The eyes, especially, get complete energy and maintain their sight. All the nerves, both efferent or afferent, get a rush of blood and as a result, sufficient energy reaches the eyes.
5. Because of the overflow of blood into the brain, the brain cells get required quantum of energy.
6. When the Guru sits under the tree, it is very beneficial because in such a position, the circulation and concentration of cosmic energy over the body of the person doing the Sastang Pranam becomes very intense and, as a result, the whole body and mind is energized and spiritized. It works in the way a elevated structure works. In the same way, the pyramidic structure of buildings like temples, churches and other religious places are also very beneficial because of fullness of concentration and condensation of cosmic energy. So, such structures are prescribed in every tradition of spirituality.

Genuflection (jaanunaman)

It is also a very scientific way of salutation. It is another way of Dandvat pranaam or prostration. While coming back to normal standing position after prostration, it comes as a link posture, but it is practised freely too.

Benefits It also gives all the benefits as mentioned in the case of Dandvat. Yes, the benefits are very intense and effective. Ordinarily, 30% blood is stored in the liver, 28% in the heart and 14% in the intestines, 14% blood in head and brain and the rest 14% is in other parts of the body. In such a posture, the percentage of blood in the head and brain is increased almost by 28% to 30%. So, this huge quantum of blood rejuvenates the whole brain and gives stamina to the eyes and ears, every cell and muscle of the face and the head. It eliminates all the ENT (problems of the eyes, nose and throat) problems. It is a most effective tool, so it is practised in every religion, traditionally.

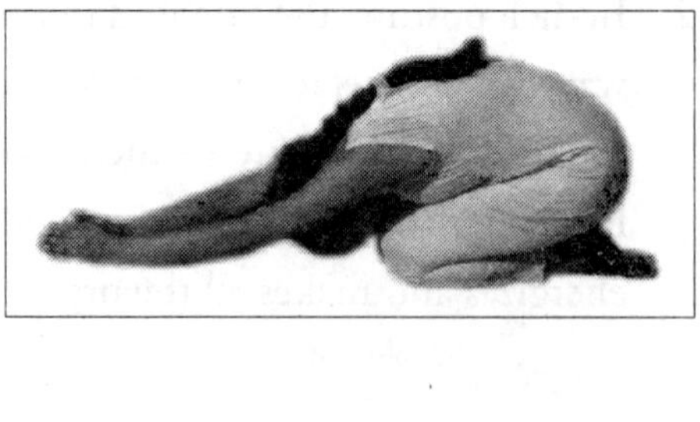

Touching feet/Charan Sparsh

This is a way to please seniors, elders and veterans. The toes are to be touched, and again the mid-point between the eyes is touched. It is a gesture in which the electro- magnetic flow of energy from the senior is collected and imbibed. The energy flows always from the toes, palms to eyes. The senior looks with the eyes, puts palm on the head of the child and the senior's toes are touched.

A scientific secret: The whole cosmos is nothing but a game of vibration of energy. Every person is part and parcel of energy. According to yogic science, our body is in the sun zone and the left part of the body is in the moon zone. Sun is the symbol of heating and moon of cooling.

The purpose of meditation is to charge the body and mind to its unlimited fullness. When anyone touches the feet of anyone, it means, the one who touches (the toucher) wants to be charged with the energy of the great sage or God-realized person (the touched) who is fully charged and able to bless one, because his electromagnetic field is so concentrated and powerful. Therefore, to touch the feet, the right toe with the right hand and left toe with the left hand is a scientific way. The action is similar to the earthing of an electric wire. It is the reason that all sages, saints give blessing with their right and hand touch with their right palm. All the gods and godess give their blessings with the right hand.

Namaste, Namaskar, Pranam

Namaste is a Sanskrit word. It is a compound word. Namah + Te. 'Namah' means to bow for paying respect and honour and 'Te' means to you. Namaste means salutation to you. In the same way, Namaskar is also a compound word. Namah + Akaar. Namah means to bow low to honour. Akaar means the figure of the person, that means bowing down for respect to your personality. Joining palms together make a circuit, which collects and absorbs the electromagnetic waves of the person who is before the doer of the Namaste.

All the four classical styles are for paying obeisance to elders. The styles of salutation are expressions of etiquette and good manners. So, sages say that children who salute and are obedient to seniors get four blessings: wisdom, long life, fame and powers. The sage says,

अभिवादनशीलस्य नित्यंवृद्धोपसेविन: ।
चत्वारि तत्र वर्धन्ते आयुर्विद्यायशोबलम् ।।

Abhivaadan Sheelasya Nityam Vridhopasevinah Chatvaritatra wardhante ayurvidya yashobalam. This means the obedient and good-mannered kid enjoys four blessings and boons–longevity, knowledge, popularity and stamina.

Punishment and Yoga

When we are talking of yoga as discipline, we must talk of punishment to instill this discipline.

The sages have specified methods and timing of punishments that can be awarded to children. Parents and teachers need to follow the rules strictly while imposing any of these four specified punishments in order to discipline a child. Just about four kinds of physical punishment is allowed.

Four kinds of punishment

1. Twisting and Pressing Ear Lobes
2. Quick Sit-Stand, Pressing Earlobes
3. Kukkut Formation
4. Canning on Palms only

Our sages gave us some specific tips to revive the enregy level and restore the psychic state and equanimity. These tips are very effective in treating excited and overflowing minds and temperamental children.

So, in the Gurukuls/ancient Indian boarding schools, all these methods were prescribed as yogic tips for treatment of the mental mechanism of children, to keep them on the right track, so that they might be mentally fit and habituated to follow a disciplined path of behaviour.

Every one likes a disciplined person, not an indisciplined one. If anyone is indisciplined, that indiscipline erupts in the mind and thereafter expresses itself in the behaviour. Sages, therefore, formulated some ways to reduce naughtiness from the psyche of children.

TIP 1

Twisting and pressing ear lobes

This is for small, mischvious kids who are between 5 to 12 years old.

When such a child is naughty, it means, his/her mind is overactive, making the kid do physiological acts of naughtiness but his intelligence is not active. The mental machinery requires sufficient energy. There is lack of life current in the brain. So, to supply energy to the brain cells for the good functioning of the brain, sages advise that the earlobes of the naughty child should be twisted for two minutes. To strengthen the intellect and subdue the mind is the purpose of this yogic tips.

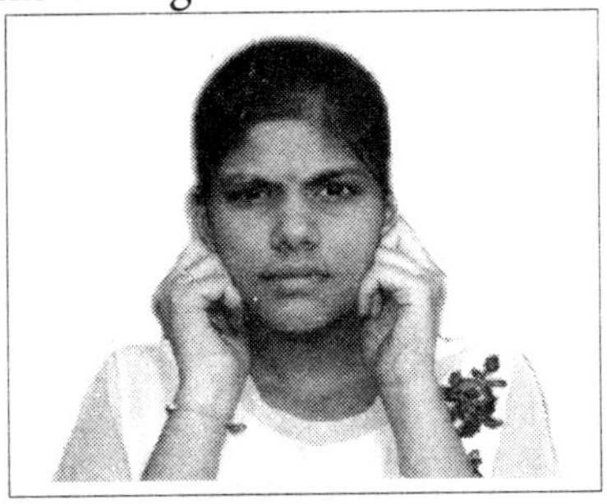

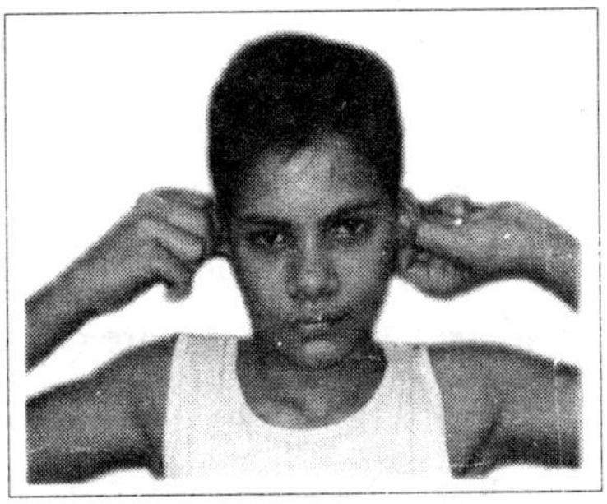

This twisting and pressing of ears of the kid is not a punishment but a treatment of the psychic fragility and mental exhaustion. It charges the brain and provides mental stamina. It activates all the mental functions and removes boredom.

You cannot just do it, however. The sages have prescribed a prescise way.

Step I

Way: Press the earlobes and pump up–not less than 60 seconds and not more than 120 seconds.

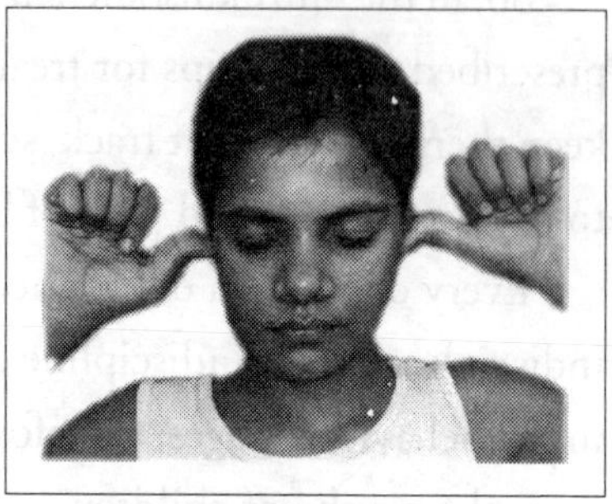

Step II

Way: Grip the whole ear and twist together in reverse way–not less than 30 seconds not more than 60 seconds.

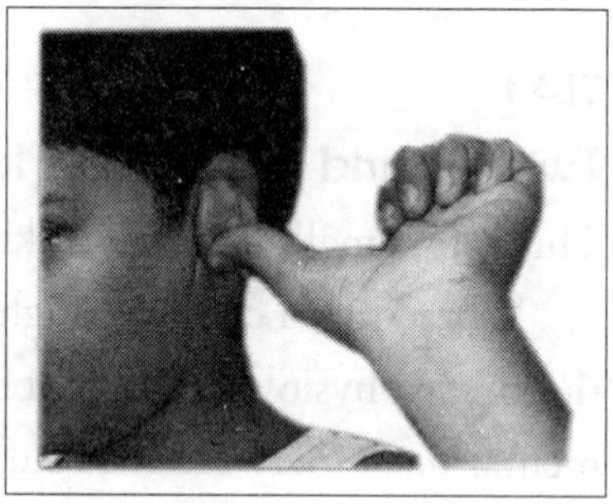

Benefits: It erases the revulsion and boredom, energizes the brain and provides stamina and interest in any mental work. It makes a child alert. It calms and cools irritation, excitement, and aggression. It brings under control a child's temper.

Step III

This is not a punishment but a yogic tip to treat the mental weaknesses of children. This tip is treatment for the nursery or primary level students. They do not require beating or caning. Only this process is sufficient to treat them in the primary stage.

Way: Cover the ear holes with the earlobes and, covering the upper part of ear, press the whole ear–not less than 30 seconds and not more than 60 seconds. At last rub the whole ear. The child will be energized, calmed and cooled. The child gets a balanced state of mind.

Note: If any teacher or parent gets angry at the naughtiness of children, then they must treat themselves first and foremost, before they think of treating the child. They must remember that punishment in yoga is not torturing, harassment or embarrassment but just treatment. The maintenance of discipline at the individual level and in society is the purpose of yoga and meditation.

Tip 2

Quickly sit down and stand up, pressing earlobes

In the Gurukuls, children were punished when they erred or broke the norms and discipline of the class. Even now, in some schools of India and abroad, children are made to do sit ups. The practice is backed by scientific and a purely yogic approach.

Why does a child play truant? Because, his energy level from head to heel is less than required. The mental mechanism of the kid is in disorder. It is because the brain does not function properly and the child loses his/her mental balance. In such a retarded condition, the child requires a balanced flow of energy. So this process is prescribed, and the child recuperates immediately, within 12 seconds. Within 12 seconds, the child feels relaxed in the legs and waist. The child pays attention in class and maintains the decorum of the class. Physiologically, the blood circulation is accelerated and oxygenation is also prompted. In this way, the whole body gets vitalized and energized. Every cell of the body is charged. It is the out come of this punishment or treatment.

This is a boon for children. So the teachers must let children enjoy this process after every period/class session. The teacher must start first and lead the kids in the class, with enthusiasm. Whenever the teacher finds children yawning and paying no attention, the teacher must bring their focus back.The teacher must get the class to do this sit down, stand up exercise to boost stamina and freshness. It is an essential exercise for children.

Step I

Way: Press the earlobes, sit and stand quickly at least 12 times.

Step II

This is only for boys.

Way: Press the upper parts of the ears, not the earlobes and sit-stand quickly at least 12 times. The second step is for those children who are victim of hydrocele (a pathological condition) or prone to it. It is a remedy for this problem. Step II is no longer in use now, though how to do it is known. No one knows the importance and efficacy of it. Only Step I is in current use. Children suffering from hydrocele should do it.

Tip 3

Kukkut Position

This method is most effective to maintain brain power and memory. It also protects children from ENT problems. It is very beneficial for the eyes. It protects the eyes and maintains sight. It gives great benefit in a little time. Sages, therefore, prescribed it in the Gurukuls for the treatment of children, to stimulate them mentally.

Here the head is bowed to the knee, and the earlobes are acu-pressed. The

posture is like being a cock. Blood rushes to the head and the neurons are energized. Brain power and memory are sharpened as a result. It makes children much more efficient. The exercise is beneficial for depressed and frustrated youth.

(1) **Way:** Stand erected, open eyes.
Breathing: Inhale long and deep at least 24 times.
Duration: 48 seconds.
Concentration–on incoming and outgoing breaths.

(2) **Way:** Bow down to the knees and keep the palms on the ground. If not possible, then touch with fingers. By practice, flexibility of toes will be maintained.
Breathing: Inhale and exhale 12 times.
Duration: 24 second only.
Concentration: Between both the eyebrows or on the third eye.
Benefit: Energization, rejuvenation of total mental mechanism.

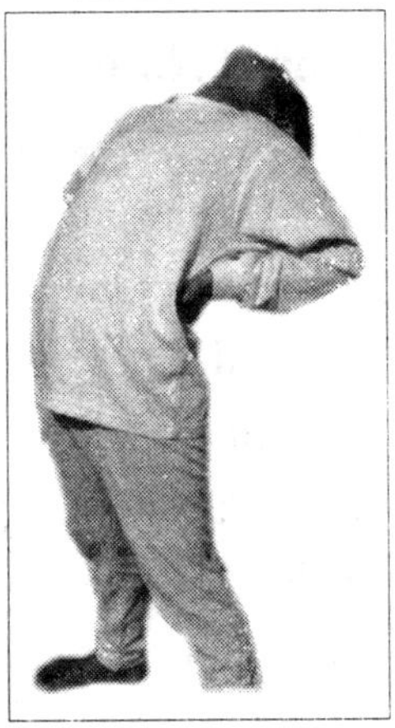

(3) **Way:** Come back and take rest for 12 breaths. Thereafter, keep the palms in the waist and bend back, rest and breath 12 times in back bent position This is the reverse of front bending. It is a must to balance the stretching of the spinal cord, as well as to maintain its flexibility. As a result, a smooth and relaxed spine provides activity and agility to the body and mind of the children. Overall, it stimulates the mind for study and work.

(4) **Way:** Bow down to the knee and, with both hands behind the thighs, acu-catch and acu-press the earlobes.
Duration: 24 seconds atleast.
Breathing: Breathing long and deep.
Benefit: It provides fullness of blood in the whole head portion, maintains the health of the ear, nose and throat and avoids mental retardation, boredom.

Tip 4

Caning on palms only

Even Today, caning is a tradition in many schools. It is very scientific if followed properly. Between the middle and ring finger, there is a point of the thymus gland, which is very important for the development of the physique of children, in a balanced way. The hormones secreted by this gland are responsible for the height and good growth of children. So, this gland is to be treated very carefully. Caning in a precise manner has been recommended to activate this gland.

This is not a punishment but treatment because this gland can be activated only when an individual is in teenage. So it is only for children.

Special Note

Teachers must strike the stick only on the palms and not on any other part or organ of the body.

Teachers must be very calm and in a cool state of mind. Not angry.

All the four punishments are to treat children, not to hurt, fracture or torture them in any way. Some children are very clever, they think it is better to suffer the sticks on the palms than to study or do home work. Such kids are always ready to be beaten or caned, but not for correction of their tendency. Teachers must not cane or hit such children.

Instead of caning, the teacher must use all the other ways of treatment, like earlobe pressing, quick sit and stand, kukkut formation (cock postures) etc, to bring behaviour change in the child.

It is the teacher's duty to inculcate love into children and motivate them to study for a good future and career. So, according to the tendency and inclination of the child, the treatment should be given. It is the failure of the teacher, if any child is detracted from the path of obedience and learning. The teacher must never loose his/her temper. The teacher must remain equipoised while treating children, because the treatment is to keep children on the anvil, not to make them afraid of study.

Yoga and Drinking Water

In the morning, after cleaning mouth and teeth, the child must take water as much as he/she can take.

Yes, water must be put in the night in a copper jug and that is to be taken in the morning. This water purifies each and every cell and nerve of the body. This copper-charged water kills all the virus in the body and protects from any viral infection. When the child drinks this water, first it goes to the mouth and kills all the germs within the mouth. Then, killing germs and virus of the gullet, it reaches in the stomach and kills all the virus. In the same way, it goes further into the duodenum, intestines and at last cleans up the whole inner metabolic mechanism.

In this duration, half of the water is digested and dissolved into blood and that blood reaches into each and every cell and

1. Salivery gland
2. Gallet
3. Stomach
4. Duodenum
5. Pancreas
6. Big intestine
7. Small intestine
9. Gallbladder
10. Liver
11. Anus

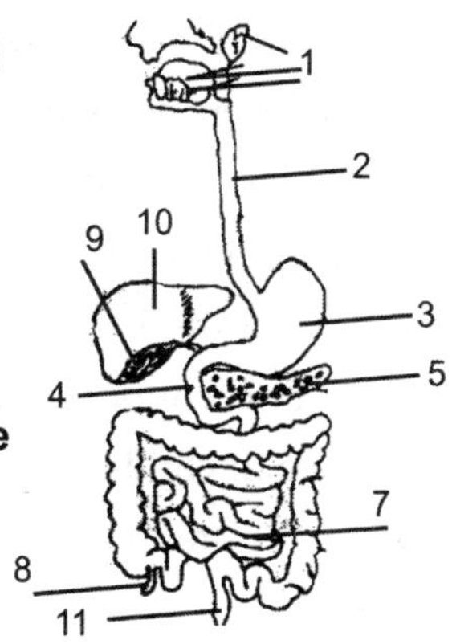

purifies the whole body. In this way, water gives immunity and disinfection to children and protects their health in every way.

❖ A child must never take water just after meals.

It is very harmful for the health. Bad health means the lack of awareness and caution, and bad life style. It is necessary to avoid all ill habits which violate decorum and discipline of the body and mind.

The water discipline is quite scientifically grounded. When one eats something, that food goes to the stomach and rests there at least for one hour. During this one hour of resting, enzymization takes place. It means all the digestive enzymes secrete from the several glands to digest the food. Respective enzymes digest respective food components. When there is water in the stomach, the enzymes get diluted and the digestive function does not happen properly.

Drinking water just after meals results in acidity, obestity, liver problems, arthritis, heart disease etc. Overall, a person gets weak and ill. The water in copper jug/pot becomes bactericidal and increases immunity of the user.

So, after a meal, one must wait for at least for one hour before drinking water. After one hour, water is necessary to liquidize the digested matter. The food takes three hours to fully digest. In the first hour it is enzymed in the stomach and then, in the second hour, it is in the small instestine. In the third hour, it is in the big intestine which absorbs all the essentials of the food.

It is good not to take water in the first hour after eating. Let the food be digested by enzymes and after one hour, enjoy drinking water. Yes, if in-between eating, water is needed, then a mere half glass of water may be taken so that the mouth and gullet is rinsed and food materials reach the stomach. The caution and precaution of drinking water are very necessary in order to maintain good health. This copper-charged water is very good for the stamina and to build resistance in children.

Note In winter, mix some boiled water to make it mild. Never take very cold water.

Yoga, Sleep and Wakening

Never sleep at sun rise.

Not only sleeping, but lying at that time is also not good for health.

In the same way, don't sleep or read at sun set.

- Always wake up before sun rise and start the daily routine. Rising and setting sun radiates ultraviolet rays which are very detrimental to health. So, it is necessary to follow the way of discipline. Wake up and wait for the sun.
- Never do yoga practice in the direction of the South.
- Never take food in the direction of the South.
- Never take lunch or dinner in a standing position. Take food always sitting, and in a leisurely manner.
- In the same way, never sit for study in the direction of the South. Sit for study facing the East or North.
- To sleep, the bed must be in the direction of the East, the head should be towards the South or East.
- Never keep your head in the direction of the North because the North pole is very powerful. There is a magnetic attraction, which interrupts the natural function of the body and brain. In course of time, children become physically exhausted, mentally retarded and dull, if they sleep with head towards the North.

Yoga, Kids and Obesity

Obesity is a big problem for modern children.It is an international problem. This is not curable through medical science. Many children are medically fit but they look very odd and awkward in size and shape. They are quite abnormal. This condition is often caused by unlaborious life style, glutenous habits and indisciplined daily routine.

Follow the way of yoga to be healthy and happy.

Science tells us, when the parathyroid gland gets damaged due to over burden of fat and minerals like calcium etc, the symptoms show themselves as fatness in tender age and as arthrits in old age.

- Children should be physically hardworking, avoid junk food and fast foods. Do yoga as prescribed for each one. Should practice all the acu-pressur tips, at the point of parathyroid gland, at least for 120 seconds three times in a day, for 60 days continuously.

  The way to control obesity is only through yoga, meditation, nature cure and nothing else. So just be aware and conscious about your health.
- When a child or young adult, even an adult, decides to do any activity that involves moving or lifting any weight, that person must make himself/herself 'airtight'.

  This means, the body should not be breathing out at that time. So, the individual must first inhale and stop the air within the body, and then move the weight. Whether the activity is kicking a bike or scooter to start it or bathing or swimming, first one must inhale and hold the breath.
- When you pour water over your head and body, first take in and hold the air within your body and then pour water over yourself. Doing so makes the nervous system strong. All these tips are to increase stamina, longevity and for a life without illness.

Yoga, Kids and Massage

It is the duty of mothers to massage their children until they become five years old. If the mother has not done this in infancy or within five years of age, the massage can even be begun when the child is a teenager.

- The teenager must massage every morning, his/her hands and feet if it is not possible to massage the whole body. The massage must begin from the elbow, via the wrist to palms and finger tips. From the knees, downward to the toes and tips of the sole. This massage is very beneficial.

  All the glandular points are either in the palms or soles.

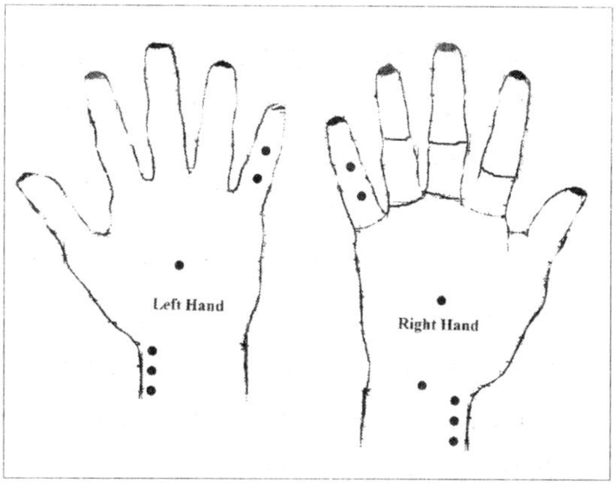

The body is to be massaged with mustard, coconut, olive or almond oil and one must bask in sunlight for at least one hour after application of the oil.

These points and glands must be stimulated through massage with mustard, coconut, olive, almond or sesame oils. This massage protects people from sexual fragility: sexual weakness in males and ovary and uterus problems in females.

Today's children are tomorrow's parents. They must be healthy and capable. Starting of this awareness must be now and today.

- For neuro and muscle weaknesses of procreative organs, massage from elbow to finger tips via wrist and palms is very important. This should be done for at least two minutes in case of male children, to facilitate their growth into healthy adults.
- In the same way, the menstrual problem of young girls is cured–whether it is a case of irregular and painful MC or leucorrhoea.

Throughe massaging of elbows, wrists, palms and finger tips, the procreative system and functions remain in order. So, for both, growing boys and girls, massaging of hands and feet in the morning and evening, is a must.

It is very beneficial, especially for the girl child.

Yoga, Awareness and Daily Life

- Never take too cold water from the refrigerator.
- Never take too hot tea, coffee or milk.
- Never take cold things after hot thing. Otherwise, teeth will become weak.
- Whenever you wake up in the morning, do not stand up from the bed all

of sudden. First sit for sometime, rub your eyes nicely, check the nostrils as to feel which nostril is open, release breath out and take it in. That is, do not jump out of bed. Sit up, exhale and inhale. If the right nostril is open and you are breathing in and out through the right of the nose, then put the right toe down first on the ground. If the left nostril is open, then put the left foot first on the ground.

- Before rubbing your eyes with palms, rub your palms together first and also clap. It would energize the eyes and the whole nervous system and will stimulate the inner organs.
- While eating don't talk, don't laugh. Eat peacefully, not angrily or when irritated.

Yoga and Siesta

After meals in the day, one must either take rest or work.

Rest is for the sick, the weak or older persons. Healthy, smart kids must work according to their priority of career or profession.

- Rest after lunch but walk after dinner.

Way: Rest–First five minutes lie straight. After five minutes, take a left turn and stay in this position for ten minutes. Then take right turn for five minutes. Then lie straight until the rest time is over. This is the scientific way of resting after meals. But only in the day time, not in night. A total of 25 minute's rest is allowed.

While turning to the left, the liver and gall bladder get opportunity to function well and release bile sufficiently, according to the quantum of food in stomach. If the left turn is not taken, and the right turn is taken first or the belly or topsy turvy position of lying occurs, this proves harmful to the process of digestion.

When the left turn is taken during afternoon rest, the breath comes in and goes out through right nostril, which increases heat within the body. This heat is very beneficial for the digestive system.

- At night, at least a minimum of 100 steps, and maximum 1,000 steps of walking is necessary.

This is very good for the discipline of the digestive metabolism. All the enzymes get to act and assimilation takes place. Walk is a must because, at night, the heat within the body is reduced. It is necessary to increase this heat. In the night the temperature cools down outside as well as within the body. So through walking, the temperature is increased within the body to maintain the normalcy and is supportive to good digestion.

Yoga and Bed Wetting

Many children pass urine in bed while sleeping in the night. This is a disorder of the nervous system and a fragile mental mechanism. In such cases, the control mechanism does not work during sleep.

There are specific reasons for dysfunctioning of the urinary mechanism. It is caused by the mialfunction of the nerves and organs.

- Continuous acu-pressure on the special points, at least for 60 days, thrice in a day, is a must to cure this problem. Within 15 days, children, both male and female, show positive results.

Way: Acupress every point at least 120 seconds each, sitting meditatively. Before acupressure, inhale and exhale 48 times deeply.

Equipment for Yoga

Proper place, time, age, diet and dress, Yoga mat, cotton bed/couch/seat, blanket are required.

Place The room must be a well ventilated room and the atmosphere should be pure, so that fresh air is available. The room and surroundings should be full of oxygen. It is best to practise this yoga at a river bank, sea shore or garden.

Time Yoga is to be done between 4 am to 8am in the morning. This is known as the Brahmamuhurt or the auspicious time. Before sun rise and after sun set are the best times to practise Yoga.

Age Yoga can be practised by all age groups, male and female. Any boy and girl aged 6 to 8 years can practice yoga.

Diet It is an important factor for yoga. The diet for a yoga practitioner should be very light and digestible. No heavy food should be consumed. It is recommended that a diet of fruits and vegetables is taken by yoga practitioners.

Dress It must be very comfortable, loose, and clean. In winter season some woolen dress, track suit must be used.

Yoga mat or cotton bed The bed for yoga practice should not be very hard. There must be a cotton matress or yoga mat on the ground or the hard bed. Otherwise, bones in the body may get hurt.

Avoid

1. Don't practice yoga just after meals. Wait at least 3 to 4 hours, except for Hasayam yoga or laughter.
2. Don't eat or drink just after yoga practice.
3. Wait at least 40 to 60 minutes.
4. Don't do yoga in haste. Do not rush or hurry through it.
5. Don't begin with meditation or Pranayama. First practise Asana, then Pranayama and thereafter, meditation, step by step, systematically.
6. Avoid wrong yoga practice. Take counsel of a yoga teacher.
7. Don't talk or laugh while practizing yoga, except for Hasayam.
8. Start with Shavasana and end with Shavasana.

Height plus Weight

Weigh yourself and maintain a proportionate weight, according to height. This is also discipline. Every child must be awere of fatness and obesity, in order to maintain the equanimity of height and weight.

	Height	Weight in kg
Male	5'5" –10	60–65
Female	5'5" –10	55–60
Male	6'5" –10	70–75
Female	6'5" –10	60–65

1. Formula:

   To lose fat—

   *3/4 spoonful of honey, not more than 30 gms. Mix into a glass of water that is not too hot, nor too cold and drink in the morning.

   If lemon suits a person, then dilute it with 2 spoonfuls of lemon juice

2. Formula:

   *3/4 spoonful honey mixed in 60 ml cow urine. Mix 2/3 spoonful of lemon juice. Drink in the morning, in empty stomach. Do not eat or drink anything at least one hour after taking this.

ॐ ॐ ॐ

Three

Yoga for Eyes

Care and Nutrition

All of us know very well how important eyes are for us. There is no life without eyes. With the help of eyes, we see every thing and do all the work in the world with happiness and zeal. There is also an adage that "care is better than cure".

If one knows how to care for the eyes and protect eye sight, one can do without eye glasses. Some cautions and precautions, along with proper nutrition, can protect the eyes. It is shocking that 3-year-old children have to wear spectacles these days.

Here, this chapter concentrates on the eyes, but the yoga for eyes also covers all the connected and respective organs near the eyes.

Tips for Eye Care

Tip 1: Fill your mouth with water. Fill the cup of the hand with fresh water and splash this water over closed eyes, one by one, by hand, after every couple of hours. This is very good for students and mental workers or workers using their eyes, users of computers. This provides coolness and well- being to the eyes.

The splash of water reduces over-heating of the eyes and a mouth full of water also supports the process of reducing temperature of the eyes. Whenever you take bath, first of all, wash your eyes, the head portion, face, neck, throat with a light massage and then pour the water over the whole body.

Tip 2: After sleep do not stand up all of a sudden. First sit erect in the bed for at least five minutes, then rub the eyes with two index fingers. It removes the blocks around eyes, and activates the muscles and nerves. Massage the palms against each other and then rub the whole head portion, neck, face, throat, yawn and stretch the body, right and left, back and front, then leave the bed.

Tip 3: Watch television from a reasonable distance, at least 3 meters away from the TV set. Never watch TV in a dark room, always have a light on.

Tip 4: Blink eyes one by one, in a cup of rose water or cold fresh water for 6 to 120 seconds.

Tip 5: Use soot or 'Kajal' in the eyes, when going to sleep. This is made of cow ghee or mustards oil, traditionally this is prepared in every home in India. It is an Ayurvedic formula to help sharpen eye sight. This protects the eye from infections and also makes the eyes healthy, clear and charming.

Tip 6: Protect the eyes from scorching rays of the sun or extreme light. Always avoid focussing on the dazzle. Use sunglasses, dark glasses when you go to the hills as there are radiations from snow in sun light.

Nutrition Tips

Tip 1: Take cow milk, which is very nutritious, especially for eyes. It increases the visual strength. It maintains youthfullness. Cow milk is full of keratin, the yellow substance is the vitamins in the milk. It gives nutrition and nourishment to the eyes.

Tip 2: Cow urine contains copper, which transforms into gold in the human body. Gold has the power to destroy all type of weakness. So it is an antidote. It makes the eyes potent. It is very nutritious for eyes and brain.

Quantity 30ml to 50 ml for adults.
20 to 30 ml for children.

Note Take it in the morning, in empty stomach.

Tip 3: Just as cow milk is the best source of keratin, which is an important substance for the nutrition, cow curd, cow ghee and all cow milk products are very good for human health.

Tip 4: All the dry fruits are very nutritious for the body. They contain fat, protein and omega 6, which are very beneficial to eye sight and memory. Omega 6 is a component that strengthens the mental mechanism. Dry fruits are costly fruits. Groundnuts are also full of omega 6 and are very cheap, not as costly as almond, cashew nuts etc. So groundnuts are the nutritional substitute for good health of eyes and brain.

Tip 5: Carrot is a good source of vitamin A or keratin and is very nutritious for the eyes. Amla is very good in any form. Whether that is pulverized or raw, or as pickle or as jam or juice. Besides all these, all the green vegetables are very good for the total health and for the eyes.

Tip 6: First knuckle of index and middle finger is the point which correspond to eyes and is related to maintaining sight. Each morning and evening, acupressure on the middle and index fingers of both the hands with each of the knuckle, should be given for 120 seconds at least. Before the acupressure on the knuckles, both the palms must be rubbed against each other and thereafter, acupressure is done.

This protects the eyes from any type of infection. This process of acupressure sends the total energy with great force into the eyes. This gives clear sight. It removes the tiredness of eyes. In the morning, to walk barefoot on frost-moist grass is very good for the eyes. It cools the eyes and mind.

Tip 7: Protect the eyes from scorching rays of the sun or extreme light. Always avoid focussing on the glare. Use sunglasses, dark glasses when you go to the hills.

Value of Eyes Exercises

Lack of energy in the eyes is the cause of poor sight. The weakness at last results in blindness. If the eyes are weak, it means lack of energy in the eyes and lack of nutrition for the eyes especially. Some times, there is plenty of energy and vitamins within the body but that energy does not reach the eyes and is unable to care for and cure the eyes in a proper way. In order to protect the eyes, it is very necessary to overhaul all the nerves which are responsible for sending energy and vitamins to the eyes.

So invigorating the nervous system is a must in order to promote the flow of blood, oxygen, vitamins to the eyes, which protect the eyes and the visual mechanism. Though the body has sufficient energy, that energy does not necessarily go the eyes. So, there are some specific exercises to send the blood into the eyes and create the supportive environment for well- being of the eyes.

After long research and many experiments, a hit formula, especially for the good of the eyes, has been found. The exercises are very effective in supplying sufficient nutrition, energy and vitamins to the eyes. The exercises break all the barriers between the eyes and the heart. The exercises remove all the toxic blocks in the veins and arteries for supply of blood to the eyes.

For example, when we sleep in the night and wake up in the morning, we find that our eyes are not able to see clearly. We find our eyes are dazzled. What do we do then? We rub them, give a light massage, and remove the toxic materials which are blocks. Clearly, this is due to functionless-ness and inactivity in the eyes through the night. When we rub our eyes, what happens? Unconsciously, we do yoga and activated the eyes. The eyes get energy and stamina. So, yoga formulations for the eyes are very scientific and effective for the eyes.

In the body, blood circulation is very important to maintain good health of the physique and the psyche, for all organs and for the eyes.

Regular practice of the formulations given below is beneficial for the eyes. The specific postures, the specific exercises are done, providing all the positive energies not only for the eyes but also for the mental mechanism and ears, nose, throat too. All the exercises are well researched and results of years of experimentation.

Preliminary Exercises for Eyes

The **Kukkut Kriyas** (for 7 to 10 minutes time duration)

This formulation is a standing exercise. It is suitable for those who go on morning walks in a park or garden. They can practice this in a standing position, on the green grass in open air.

It is very easy to perform. It is said to be a hi-tech formulation because, it gives a great deal of benefits within a short time. Today, when everything is hi-tech, why not yoga?

For eye care and cure, this hi tech formulation gives benefits to the practitioner in minimum time. Yoga is a prevention and prevention is first-aid. All the preventive efforts are for care and awareness. In the case of eyes, the critical condition is thick glasses with very high lense power. At the end is blindness.

The prevention is to reduce the power of the lense in the eye glass. It is necessary to practise this formulation along with the tips for eye care and cure, and intake of proper nutrition for the eyes. Regular exercises are a must for the prevention of any minor or mega problems related to eyes.

Exercises

Step 1

Way Stand erect, facing towards the East or North, not West or South.

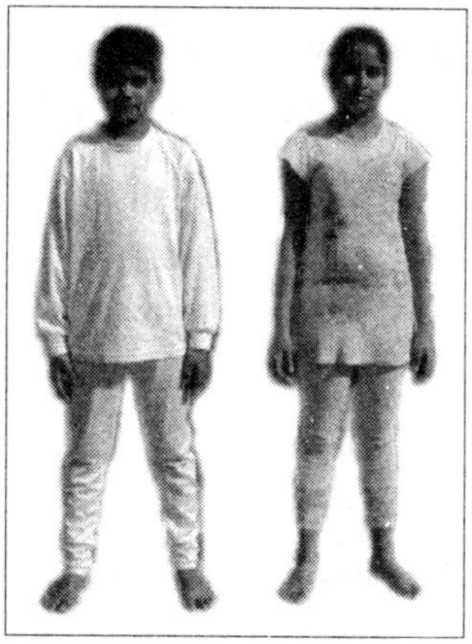

Breathing Long and deep breaths at least 120 times. At the start 60 times.

Duration 120 seconds in starting.

Benefit It normalizes the over-activation of the body. It gives relaxation to mind and body, which is the ground for the practice of further steps. This exercise is must for the beginner.

Step 2

Way Stand on tiptoes and stretch the hands towards the sky.

Breathing Inhaled breath must be held.

Duration As long as the breath can be held.

Benefit It gives stamina to the lungs. It stretches the chest, arms, neck, throat, and the whole head portion. As a result, the breathing mechanism gets strength and stamina and this relieves asthmatic problems. It energies each and every cell and nerve of the chest and the head portion.

Step 3

Way Bending the back, put the palms over the waist and bend back further and look towards the sky.

Breathing Inhale and exhale 12 times deeply.

Duration 24 seconds.

Benefit This step gives flexibility to the spine and energises the life current in the whole body mechanism. It avoids the ground for and scope of cervical spondylitis problem. It also dilates the chest, lungs, heart, stomach, liver, food pipe and breathing pipe. Overall, this step strengthens all the metabolic functions of the body.

Step 4

Way Bend forward and grip the knee caps and apply as much force as you can tolerate.
Breathing Inhale and exhale 12 times.
Duration 24 seconds at least.
Benefits It is the reverse of the previous step.

It is essential to practise it in a sequential order because it gives all the benefits only when it is practised in a sequence. It is very beneficial for the flexibility of the knees and thighs. Overall, the legs get stamina and strength.

Step 5

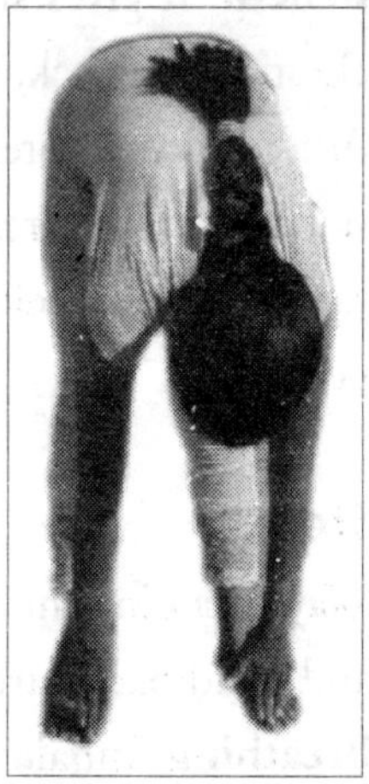

Way Now let go of the knee caps and try to touch the toes. If you cannot touch the toes in the first attempt, keep trying. Gradually this will become easy.
Breathing 12 times.
Duration 24 seconds.
Benefits It is an advanced step from the previous one. It strains the legs and at last, gives relaxation and makes the legs flexible.

Step 6

Way Put the palms over the waist and twist to backside, via left and right sides.
Breathing Stay in twisted position and take long and deep breaths 12 times.
Duration 24 seconds.
Benefits It is very good for the flexibility of the waist and the spinal cord at

the same time. It removes the tenseness of the sciatic nerve and relieves sciatic pain in course of time. It has a very positive effect on heart, lungs and liver.

Step 7

Way Put the palms over waist and bend to right, and later on to left side.

Breathing Deep breath at least 12 times.

Duration 24 seconds on each side. 48 seconds on both the sides.

Benefits It maintains the flexibility of the waist and the rib-cage on both sides, left and right. It eliminates the scope of fat storage in the waist. All the nerves related to the spine get relaxed.

Step 8

Way Bow down, forward and bring the face close to the knees and press the ear lobes. The legs must be straight.

Breathing Breathing should be quite normal.

Duration Each exercise takes 40 to 60 seconds at least.

Benefits It is very beneficial for the eyes and brain at the same time. It gives all the genuflective benefits. When earlobes are pressed, immediately it removes all the sloth and boredom. It enhances interest and liking for study and mental work. It sharpens the comprehensive capacity of the practitioner. This is the essence of this advance exercises. It provides all the positive effects to the eyes, brain, ears, face, throat, teeth and so on. Overall, the whole head portion gets blood in sufficient quantity

Step 9

Way This is the Kukkut Asan, the final step of this formulation.

All the advanced eye exercises are to be applied here, in this physical position. After doing eye exercises, come back and stand straight.

Breathing Long and deep at least 60 times.

Duration 40 to 60 seconds at least.

Benefits It relaxes the whole body. It is a standing Shawasana. It brings all the harmonious state to the mind and the body.

Note After 120 seconds, massage all over the head portion and, especially the eyes. Rubbing and massaging should be done for at least 60 seconds. The massage and then, pressing the temple and the eyes massage should be done carefully.

This process can be repeated at least two times more. In total, it must only be thrice and not more than three times. It should be done in the morning. If it is done in the evening, then again, the massage should be repeated not more than three times.

Advanced Eyes Exercises

(1) **Way** Move the pupils in the right and the left direction, without moving the head.
Breathing Breathing should be normal.
Duration 6 to 8 seconds, then relax.

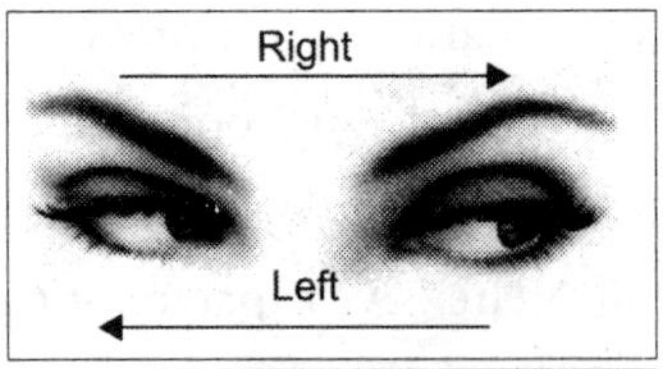

(2) **Way** Move the pupils towards the chin and then upward towards the top of the head, step by step.
Duration 6 to 8 seconds, then relax.

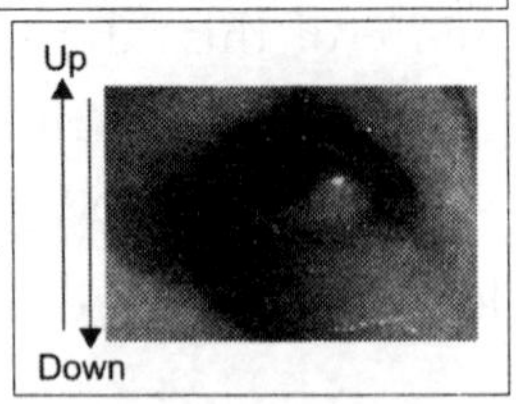

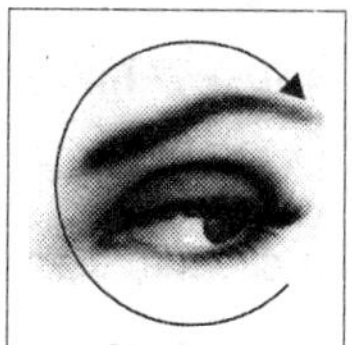
Clock wise

(3) **Way** Move the pupils clock wise.
Duration 6 to 8 seconds then relax.

(4) **Way** Move the pupils anti-clockwise.
Duration 6 to 8 seconds then relax.

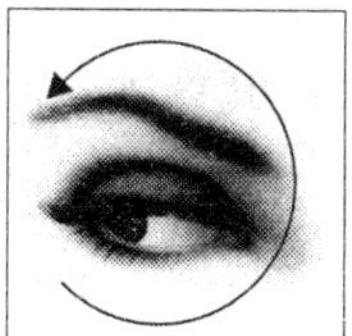
Anti-clock wise

(5) **Way** Close the eye lids forcefully, open and dilate the pupils, with the help of fingers.
Duration 6 to 8 seconds, then relax.

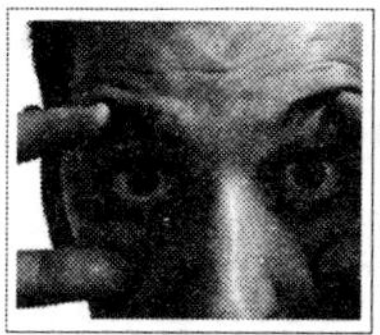

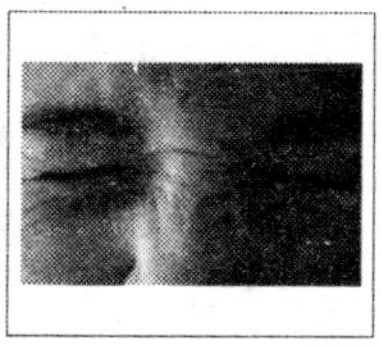

(6) **Way** Put the tip of the thumb to the temples and press at least 6 to 10 seconds, and move the mouth as if munching something.

Note All these steps are to be applied while in the cock posture.

Benifits This package is based on physio-therapeutic maneuvers and is the positive results of an anatomical approach. So this yoga give quite positive results after gradual and sequential practice of all the exercises within the package. Within 60 days, the practitioner gets rid of his spectacles or eye glasses. If an individual is in good health and practises daily, then his eyes will never be weak.

This package heals the eyes and promotes all the supportive functions within the body mechanism, whether this is neural, hormonal, nervous, vital or spinal.

The genuflection and Dandvat postures are very important in order to energise the eyes. In such postures, the blood reaches the upper part of the body to heal the heart, lungs, liver, throat and head portion. The blood rushes towards head and brain in huge quantum.

If the percentage of the blood in the portion of the head, brain and eyes is reduced, this causes headache, irritation, tension, depression and aggression takes place, and the individual is considered 'not cool' and not sober. When the head portion is filled with sufficient quantity of blood and the eyes get energy and the brain cells also get charged, then the practitioner becomes a cool and calm person, having a keen eye sight.

Continuous tension and depression leads to weak eyes. If the head is not good, then the eyes also cannot be good and the ears, nose, face, throat also get affected.

This package covers all the root causes of problems of the eyes and brain. Due to the specific posture, the percentage of blood increases in the head portion. An increase from 14% to 28 or 30% rejuvenates all the brain cells, neurons, eyes, ears, every cell and muscles of the face. As a result, the face acquires youthfulness and a reddish glow, is cheerful and charms. Parathyroid and thyroid glands get activated and maintain the maximum corum of health. The teeth, tongue, jaws, gums get strength. The problem of hair loss and whitening is also controled by these exercises.

The package not only protects the eyes but also the brain. The practitioner gets good mental health and eye sight and natural stamina. Yes, regular practice makes the practitioner perfect in respect of the health of ear, nose and throat too. It gives mental strength. All the benefits are gained within minutes, not hours of pain and trouble.

ॐ ॐ ॐ

FOUR

ASANA
(POSTURES)

Meaning and Motif of Asana/postures

The word Asan means a 'sitting position' of the body, which gives a sense of well being to the body and a calm mind.

The term *Asana* is used for a carpet of grass, a square piece of cloth or a mat which is a comfortable seat on the ground. In Patanjali's *Astangyoga* the term *Asana* finds third place. (1) Yam (2) Niyam and after that (3) Asan followed by (4) Pranayam.

The translation of the word *Asana* into English has been done as a posture. The word posture does not do justice to the word Asan, it does not explain the letter and the spirit of the word Asan. Posture means the common position of sitting, lying, standing or the prescribed posture for a purpose, just as for sleeping, running, working, biking, reading etc. All the postures are for normal activity or compulsive positions of body which are required for normal work, while Asanas have a therapeutic character and property.

All the Asanas have been formulated very thoughtfully. It is a deliberate treatise for our physical and mental wellbeing. All the Asanas have been formulated by the sages on the basis of physiology, anatomy and physiotherapy.

So *Asana*, posture and exercise are not synonyms. Asanas are well organized on the physiotherapeutic basis. Postures are normal physical positions. Exercises are quick and jerky movements while Asanas are practised in a very slow and relaxed manner. The exercises give tension and are tiresome, while Asanas give flexibility and relaxation for well being of the practitioner.

Maharshi Patanjali provides an aphorism to give the exact answer to the question 'what is Asana?' [स्थिरसुखमासनम्] Sthirsukhamasanam means stable and comfortable posture. This is the Asanas that gives stability and comfort. This aphorism clearifies the motif of the Asanas because all the Asanas escalate the flexibility within the body and the flexible body aquires ease and poise at a physical and mental level.

Therefore, Asanas must be practised very meditatively, not rashly. According to Patanjali, an effortless maintenance of *Asana* frees the mind to contemplate on the meditative point. It is better to meditate on God or the infinite. During Asanas, the practitioner must think about the mortality of life, and Asanas can release tension and depression.

The aim and objective of the Asanas are to make the body perform higher meditative practices. Mastery over the Asanas is possible only through a long period of time and regular practice. Then anyone can sit for hours for meditation.

To give the flexibility and stamina to the practitioner to sit for hours is the purpose of the Asanas. The capacity for sitting for hours is possible only when the body is in a good condition, the metabolic system and hormonal secretions work.

Asanas provide equilibrium over all functions in all the dimensions, whether that is emotion, behaviour and perception. The practice of Asanas promotes and maintains the healing process within the body and reconditions the body. The Asanas provide good harmony between the body and the mind. The practice of Asanas reduces stress, strain and tension due to work or due to the daily overwork.

Here, one thing is very important to note: that Asanas are used or understood in the name of yoga by the modern youth. All over the world, the word yoga is used for Asanas . The word yoga and meditation are very popular in today's world. As yoga is understood to mean Asanas, and meditation means Dhyan, the word yoga is generally used in the combined sense of *Asana* postures and exercises.

The Classification of Asanas

1. Cultural Asanas
2. Relaxing Asanas
3. Meditative Asanas

Cultural Asanas

Most of the Asanas are cultural Asanas. The characteristics of the cultural Asanas are to recondition the body and mind. All these provide correction to the wrong way of sitting, lying and working. Though the bad effects of bad postures may not have any outward expression, but the physiological and psychological conditions may be very weak and ill. Such an ill- conditioned body may not be suitable for the practice of higher techniques of Pranayam and meditation.

All the cultural Asanas are front and back bending, left and right bending, back twisting via left and right, and concern the abdomin and waist. All joints, muscles, glands, tendons, ligaments are reconditioned in full swing. The whole body gets healed and energised.

Relaxing Asanas

Relaxing Asanas are very important. All these give very deep relaxation, after the practice of all the cultural Asanas . Relaxing Asanas remove all the root causes of tension, depression, aggression or frustration of the mind and make the practitioner fit for the higher practices of Pranayam and meditation. Shawasan, Balasan and Dandvatasan are very effective relaxing Asanas.

Meditative Asanas

Meditative Asanas are the conclusion of the cultural and relaxing Asanas. In such Asanas, it is possible to achieve the benefits of trance.

They are for physio- stimulation and psycho- stimulation.

Some exercises, some formulations for the healing and overhauling of children's bodies and minds are given physio-therapeutically. All the Asanas have been formulated for the good health of children, so that they may enhance their aptitude, apprehensive capacity and their mental mechanisms may become efficient. In sum, all the formulations are based on physiotherapy and psychotherapy.

Physical-stimulation

Yoga is not only a physical exercise but it concentrates on the whole mechanism of body. The body mechanism is made of skeleton, muscles, nervous network, tissues, glands, lungs, heart, skin, brain or mental mechanism etc. The yogic concept is to energise the life current and spread it over the entire body mechanism, from the top to the bottom, from head to heel.

These days, children are keen to join gyms to build muscles, biceps, packs, to be handsome, smart and charming. They do not know the harms of gym exercises for the young body.

Yoga practices protects all parts and organs of the body, while gym exercises concentrate on only muscle building. The benefits which are expected from a gym are available through yoga practice also. Yoga cares for the all-round development of the body and the mind. All of you must know that all the benefits and achievements from a gym can be achieved through the practice of yoga also. Yoga helps develop the all- round personality, which is every child's requirement.

Gym exercises develop only the muscles of the chest, arms, thighs and belly. Through yogic tips, all the benefits are achieved without any harm.

Doctor Peter Northstron, a physiotherapy researcher, has said, "Over-laborious exercises weaken the bones of the body. Due to excess of labour, the salt and minerals within the body get eroded or reduced". So, laborious stretching exercises are very harmful for not only the bones but also the whole body.

Yoga takes care to avoid the harms first and then gives benefits. Here, some tips are prescribed for the children which give stamina and strength, causing no harm. These tips give good shape to the body and increase the glow in the skin and face, with balanced muscles and charming looks.

Tips for Cleaning of the Nose

In our body, two organs–the heart and lungs–function from mother's womb and up to the last moment of life. Both the organs never take any rest. Their functions go on throughout life, expressing itself in the form of respiration which shows, a creature is alive.

We require food twice in a day and water four or five times in a day but we require air all the time. Whether we are sleeping or awake, talking or walking, reading or running, we breath. Without breath, no one can survive even for two minutes. This important function is performed by the nose. If the nose is not cleaned, then this activity of breathing is impaired.

Both the nasal cavities must be cleaned so that pure air with oxygen gets to the lungs easily to purify the whole body. The purified body is a healthy body. In such a purified or healthy body, resides the healthy mind. So, this yoga starts with cleaning of the nose. Nasal cleanliness is the first and foremost yoga exercise. If this is not done, the complete benefits of further exercises will not acrue. Children must be taught to do this regularly.

Step 1

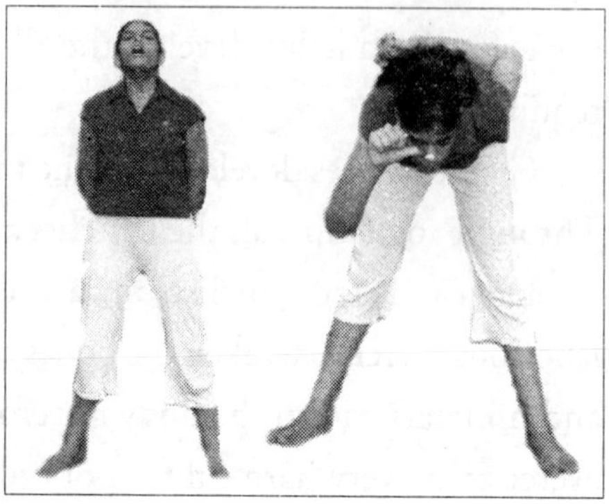

Way Stand erect. Open your mouth and inhale. Close right nasal pore with the thumb of the right hand. Bow down to the knees. Exhale out through the left nostril, forcefully. Again repeat it through the right nasal pore , using the left thumb.

Duration 12 times, one by one for each nostril.

Step 2

Way Go down on the knees and get into a kneeling position. Open the mouth like a lion. Take the tongue out, inhale through mouth. Exhale through the mouth, with force and speed. Do this 12 times. But not more than 12 and not less than 12 times. A coughing sound should emerge with every exhalation.

Note This is to be done on an empty stomach or four hours, after meals. At least 6 times, gustfully.

Benefits Without proper practice of this tip, there is no scope for further exercises as well as benefits.

Both the steps give stamina to the lungs, muscles of eyes and brain. Both protect from ENT problems, remove the scope of bronchial asthma, throat's sensitivity, sinusitis, coughing and hicups. These eradicate cold and rheumatism. While practising these yogas, our body absorbs sufficient amount fresh air, which supplies us with 'lifetron' or a vital force. These exercises provide us with physical stamina as well as mental strength. It is better to practise them in the morning, after brushing. It must be added as a daily routine of life. Then, for the whole day, sniffing or sneezing will be contained.

These exercises can be practised in the evening too. They help reduce depression, irritation and retardation. The personality develops as a positive, cooperative, supportive and tolerative person. It freshens and cleans the nasal cavity. In the evening too, it removes all the smoky and dusty particles that get struck in the nose during long working hours and commuting. Everyday, cleansing of the nostrils is a must to protect one from pollution and related breathing troubles.

Balada Kriya

Step 1

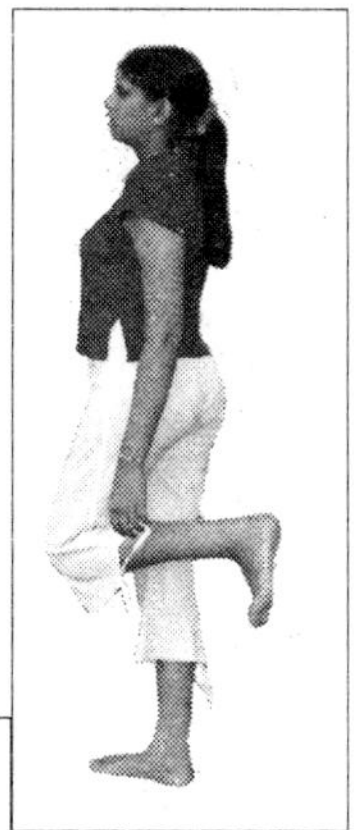

[बलं ददाति इति बलदा Balam Dadati iti Balada]. The exercise which gives a person power, strength, potency and efficiency is known as the Balada exercise. Through this exercise, the whole body gets energy and stamina.

Way Legs should turn back and heel touch hips one by one. synchronizing, with exhaling breath.

Duration 24 times totally.

Step 2

Way Make a fist with the thumb, within the fingers' clutch and close the fist. Keep the right hand straight. The left elbow should go back and fist touch the armpit. One by one, move, exhaling breath as fast as can be done.

Duration At least 24 steps

Step 3

Both the earlier steps were preparation for this final step to complete the exercise.

Way The movement of legs, hands and the exhaling of breath should occur in a synchronized manner.

Breathing Breathing should synchronize with the movement of legs and hands.

Duration Ten seconds. Not a minute. Just 10 seconds leads to decrease of exhaustion. As much as 30 seconds duration is for a complete and perfect course.

Benefits It increases the stamina, capability and strength of the physique. It is only for children and only children can do it. It gives benefits equal to one hour of morning walk or one km of running, within a span of 10 seconds. This is a hi-tech exercise , which gives great benefit in a little time. So its name is Balada Kriya hitech or strength giving exercise.

Dand Kriya

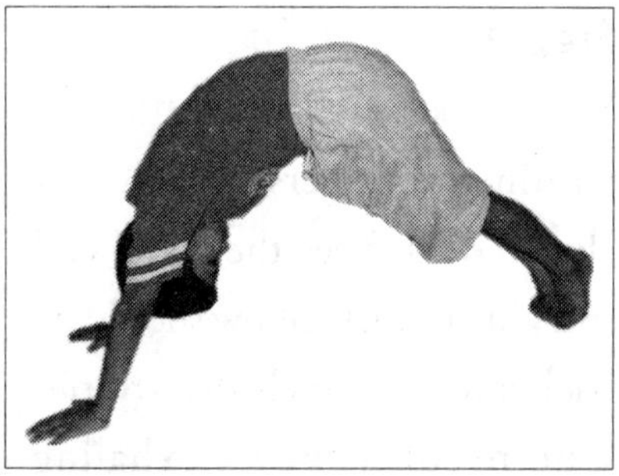

Way Lie down on the belly. Put your palms straight on the ground. Inhale and rise, to bend towards the sky. Exhale. Come back, inhale. Repeat it as much as possible. At least five times in the beginning. Gradually, more times may be added, according to the capacity.

Benefit This is the most popular exercise in India to strengthen the body. It is a very energising exercise and it gives a good shape and size to the body. It is combination of Parvatasan and Bhujangasan. Both the Asanas practiced rythmically, one by one, with increasing speed.

Dhanush Kriya Formulation

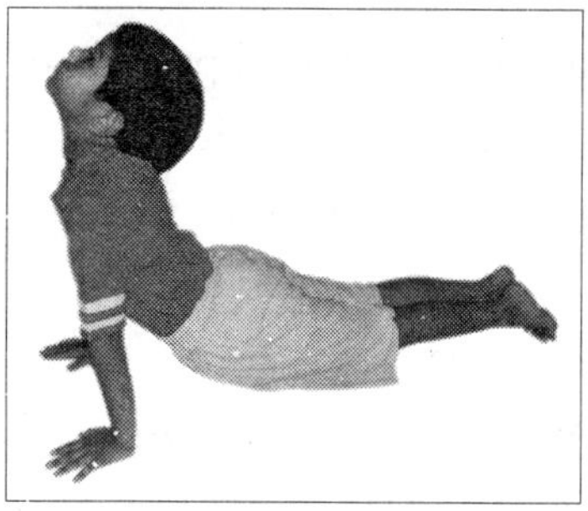

This is the formulation of seven cultural Asanas very beneficial for psychosomatic healing. This formulation gives a spurt of energy to the spine, belly, nervous network, metabolic function, blood circulation, joints, chest, throat and mental mechanism.

(1) Shawasan (2) Sarvangasan (3) Halasan (4) Bhujangasan (5) Dhanushasan (6) Balasan (7) Shawasan/Shav-asan.

Shawasan

Way Lie down in a relaxed mood. The whole body should be loose and relaxed.

Duration 2 to 3 minutes.

Concentration No concentration, just feel the in-coming and out- going breaths.

Benefits This Asanas gives complete relaxation to the body and at the mental level. Each and every organ becomes free from distress, pressure or over activity. All the visceral organs get a perfect harmony. This harmony is the basis for complete benefits of doing further Asanas Asanas .

Sarvang Asanas

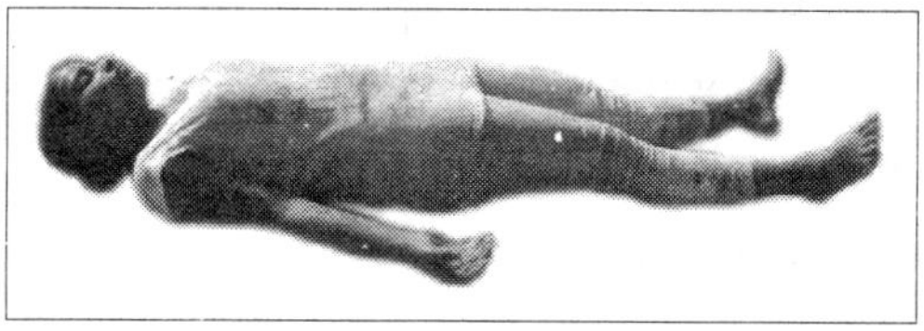

Way After Shawasan, raise your legs toward the sky and lie straight. Grip the waist with both hands. Rest in this position.

Duration 3 to 5 minutes

Concentration Straightness of legs, belly and hips.

Benefits In this position, the body becomes topsy turvy. The gravitation force runs against the body which balances organs. The organs like liver,heart, kidneys

and lungs get some pressure of gravity and a rush of blood. The gravity and pressure of blood re-conditions all the organs and energises them for their respective functions.

Halasan

Way After Sarvang Asana, bring the legs towards the head and try to put the toes on the head. The legs must be errect. It's regular practice will give perfection.

Duration 2 to 3 minutes

Concentration On the in-coming and out-going breath.

Benefits Halasan breaks barriers and creats acute pressure of blood all around the heart. It breaks the clots of cholestral and reduces the scope of hypertension, hypotension and heart or brain stroke.

Bhujang Asana

Way Lie down on the belly and put the palms beside the shoulders. Raise the chest and head towards the sky.

Duration 2 to 4 minutes .

Concentration On the breaths

Benefits It makes the spine flexible.

It stops the scope of fat increasing in the belly and waist. It stretches the ribs and lungs. This *Asana* removes tension of the sciatic nerve.

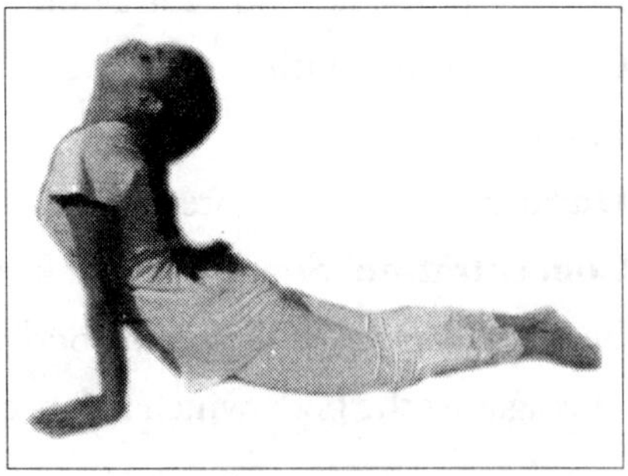

Dhanush Asana

Way See the figure carefully and copy. After Bhujang Asana, catch the ankles by the hands and raise the thighs and head,

chest at the same time in a synchronized way. Rest in that position.

Duration 40 to 60 seconds

Concentration On the breaths only.

Benefits It exerts an acute pressure on the heart, liver, lungs and belly . It gives a good massage to the intestines. As a result, this *Asana* develops the stamina for heart and other organs.

Balasan

After Dhanushasan, for better relaxation, this is a very effective Asana.

Way After Danushasan, keep the right hand and right leg straight. Right temple should touch the ground, along with the ear. Left hand and left leg should be folded towards each other.

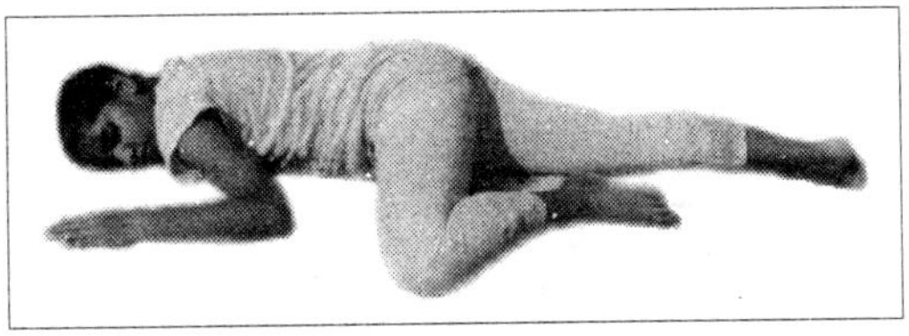

Note After Balasan, for relaxation do Shawasan, At the end, it must be done for 5 minutes, maximum for 15 minutes.

Surya Namaskriya

Surya Namaskar Asanas are ancient formulation of some exercises. The purpose of these exercises is to make flexibilize and relax the whole body and the joints.

The traditional Surya Namaskar Asanas or Sun salutations are practised in three rounds. This means that the same postures are practised three times in one set.

Surya Namaskriya is practised only once. In every set, 6 deep- breathing exercises are included. This formulation takes less time and gives more benefit. It is a hi-tech formulation, a modification of the traditional Suryanamaskar Asanas. The inclusion of 6 breathings exercises enriches this formulation with pranayamic properties. Counting the breathings provides the meditative touch to

Surya Namaskriyas

this formulation. In this way, it becomes a complete therapeutic and energizing formulation.

Note Add six long and deep breathing spans in every posture.

Height and Kids

Many children face problem of height. Though they want an appreciable height, they and their parents and teachers are not aware of what to do for children to grow tall.

There are two causes of children being short. One is genetic and the second is hormonal imbalance. There is a hormone which gives height. This hormone is in the pituitary gland, which is responsible for the height. Through practice of this yogic tip, height can be increased because the method releases the growth hormone produced by the gland. It is effective only for children. By this practice, teenageers can gain 6 inches and after the teenage, a person can gain at least 3 more inches.

Height Increasing Points

Way Sitting in meditative posture (Padmasan), clap first at least 108 times. Then acupress all the points indicated in the figure at least for 120 seconds for each, thrice in a day regularly.

Note This formula is for the children and teenagers.

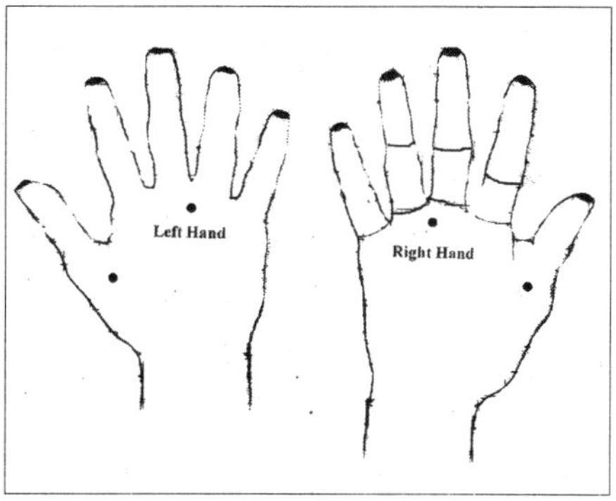

Prana Kriya

The whole world is nothing but the game of vibration of waves and rays. The whole cosmos is full of vibration of energy, which is called cosmic energy. We creatures are part and parcel of that energy. In yogic terms, this energy is called Prana or Mahaprana.

There are many methods to control this Prana at a particular point, or place. All the religious synagogues, temples, mosques, and churches are conceptualised with the idea of concentrating the cosmic energy at one place, i.e, the place of worship, to benefit human beings. In this regard, all the pyramidic structures are very therapeutic. This is the reason behind pyramidic or domed structures of for all religious and holy buildings.

The Prana Kriya is an acute way to collect and concentrate the cosmic energy into a particular part or organ of the body, to recharge the body fully. One effective tip is being given here for children.

Way Lie down on a hard bed, over a blanket. Make the pyramidic shape of the palms. Put the right hand over the navel portion and the left palm over the heart.

Duration 5 to 8 minutes.

Breathing Long and deep breathing.

Concentration Over the right pyramidic position of the palms.

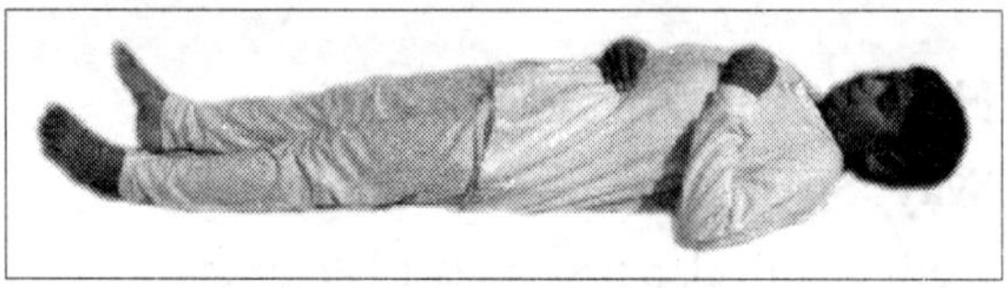

Benefits It charges each and every cell of the body. As a result of this charging, immunity of the body is increased and the body and mind get energy and ample relaxation.

Note Whichever organ requires this energy or relaxation, put the palm over that organ. Some organs require special treatment by concentration of the cosmic energy or Mahaprana through pyramidic shape of palms.

Psychological-stimulation

Today people's brain power is very weak and memory is fragile. Why is it so? In ancient India, sages had miraculous brain power and they could write so many great scriptures. Many may not believe that a mere man wrote the voluminous scriptures but the fact is, all the scriptures were written by human beings who were perfect yogis. They practised all the yoga tips and meditation.

They increased their brain power and memory and, then alone, were they able to remember all the knowledegable things that they handed down to us, much of it through memorising for generations in the not too distant a past.

The greatest epic of the world, *Mahabharat* was written by the great sage Maharshi Vedvyas. In the same way *Ramayan* was written by Maharshi Valmiki, *Charaksamhita* by Maharshi Charak, *Yoga Sutra* by Maharshi Patanjali, *Brahmsutra* by Maharshi Badarayan, *Kamsutra* by Maharshi Vatsyayan and so on. Even today, any child can be like these great sages, if he or she practises yoga tips and follows the prescriptions and injunctions.

Any child can improve his/her memory and brain power by drinking cow milk. All the Rishis and sages used to drink cow milk and looked after cows in their ashrams. Rishis and Munis prescribed some superhit yoga tips, so that in daily routine, everyone may benefit and maintain his eye sight, brain power and memory.

This is the genuflection or jaanunaman kriya. It is important. It gives much benefit within seconds. It energizes each cell of the brain and facial muscles. In this way, it avoids wrinkles on the face. Teeth get strength and ears get strong. The whole ENT system is overhauled and energized. The brain cells or neurons get full supply of energy through blood because, in such physiological position, the head is brim full of blood and it is the way to rejuvenate the mental mechanism.

The genuflection kriya gives full scope for rejuvenation because it gives pressure in the belly and forces the blood to circulate toward the head and that heals all the head nerves, cells and mental mechanism.

> ***One thing is very wonderful here. This jaanunaman kriya is even now in practice in every religious tradition, as a manner of obeisance. Hindus, Jains, Budhists Shikhs all sects genuflect in temples, offering reverence and paying obeisance. Muslims also do Namaz in this posture. Christians too bow down on Sundays while confessing before the idol of Christ. In every way of spirituality, it***

is in vogue because of it's beneficial ground and healing quality. It is a universal exercise. Rishis and sages had only prescribed it in religious rituals.

Medha Kiryas (Psychological retreat)

Step 1 Shawasan

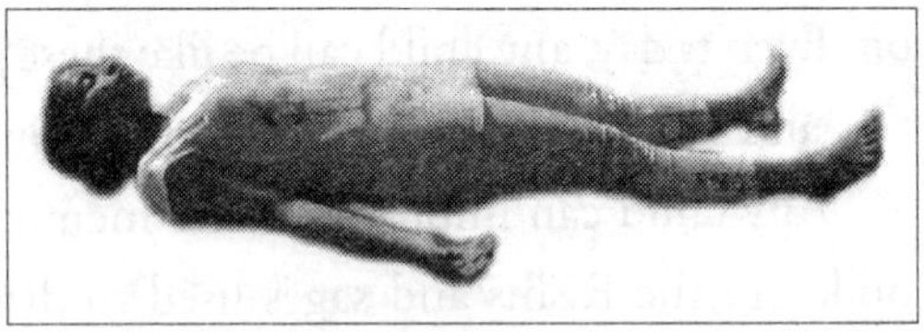

Way Lie down in a relaxed way and concentrate on the whole body for some seconds. Afterwards, engage the mind at the toes. Thereafter, gradually, move focus to the calves and shin, knees, thighs, belly, chest, throat, neck. Then to the lips, cheeks, nose, eyes, ears, forehead and the skull. After completion of the gradual concentration on all parts of the body, one by one, at last concentrate on the whole body again and then the posture is over.

Breathing Take deep and long breaths

Duration At least 2.30 minutes, not more than 5 minutes.

Benefits This posture is very necessary for the complete relaxation of the whole body because without a relaxed body and mind, if any exercise is practised, it can affect the body badly.

This exercise is started after Shawasan and finished also with Shawasan. This is the Rishic prescription. So it is not to be violated.

Step 2 Dandvatasan

Way Lie down on the belly and join the palms. Stretch the legs and palms in opposite direction to each other, forehead touchi·ng the ground.

Note A clean hanky or towel is a must under the nose and mouth, to stop dust and virus from entering into the lungs while breathing. The clean towel or hanky should be washed witn dettol.

Breathing Normal

Duration 120 seconds at least in total duration. Rise the forehead, a little, for 10 seconds, and put it down again.

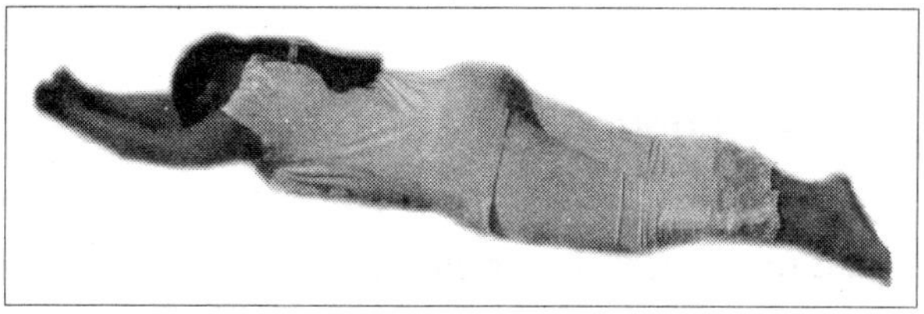

Benefits In such a posture, the upper part of the body gets opportunity to be full of blood because the gravitational force attracts all the blood particles to the ground side, where the forehead, neck, throat, eyes, ears, head, chest, shoulders are enriched with a huge quantity of blood. All the organs within the head portion are charged fully. All the organs get stamina and strength. No chance of ENT problems. Ordinarily, this part of the body never gets energy or nutrition. It is the cause of weak eyes, brain mechanism, faded face, tense mind, bald skull, weak teeth, weak ears etc. Through this posture, all such effects are negated and one acquires a healed head and happy mind.

Step 3 Sirandolani Kriya

Way Posture is the same as for Step 2. But here, the practitioner has to vibrate his/her whole head.

Breathing Normal

Duration 40 to 60 seconds and then relax.

Benefits In such a position the blood reaches each and every cell of the brain and eyes. So the energy supply becomes sufficient in quantity. The head portion, and the eyes especially, get enough energy and nutrition. This quick movement of the head breaks all the blocks and congestion in the head portion. It protects not only eyes and

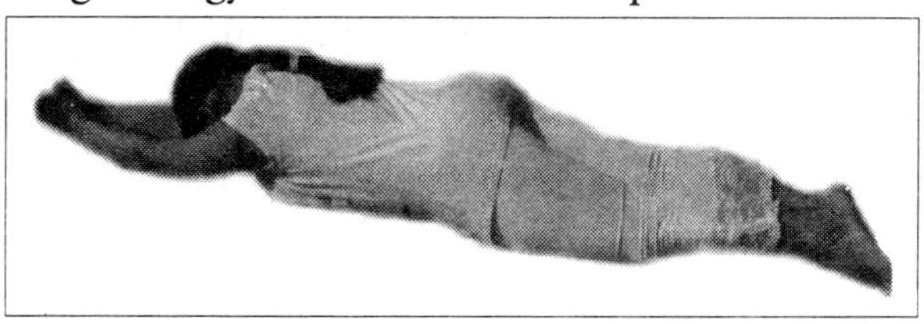

the brain, but ears, nose throat and teeth also. It provides a good scope for the access of blood into each and every cell of the ENT and mental mechanism.

Step 4 Jaanunaman Kriya (Genuflection)

Way Set the thighs (after Sirandolani Kriya) slowly against the belly. Bend the head to the ground. Stretch the hands straight.

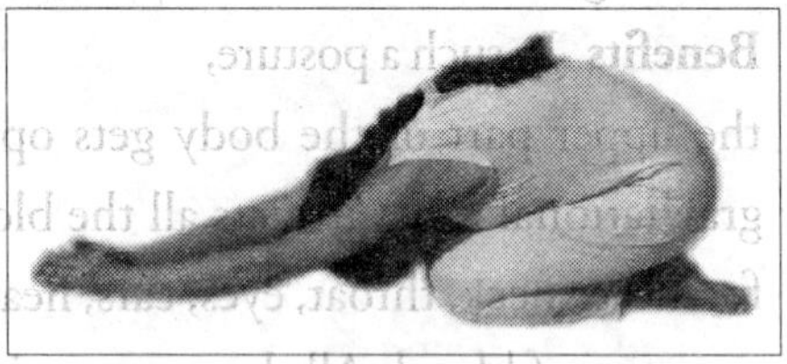

Breathing Normal.

Duration At least 40 to 60 seconds then come back and sit erect in Bajrasan for 60 to 120 seconds.

Step 5 Ustrasan

Way Keep the belly and chest forward. Hang the head behind, and grip the ankles.

Breathing Breath 12 times deeply in this position.

Duration 24 seconds only in the beginning. In the course of time not more than 120 seconds.

Concentration On spinal cord

Benefits It makes the whole spine flexible and allows the life current to flow. It strengthens the spine, stretches the lungs and energizes heart and liver.

Step 6 Bajrasan

Way Follow the picture accurately.

Note After 120 seconds, relax. Rub the palms against each other until they warm up. Give a massage all over the head portion, at least thrice. Rub the palms over face, eyes, and ears. Rub each and every root of hair on the head. At last give massage from the neck to the head and go to the forehead, face and throat at least thrice. After rubbing and massaging, sit closing the eyes for 40

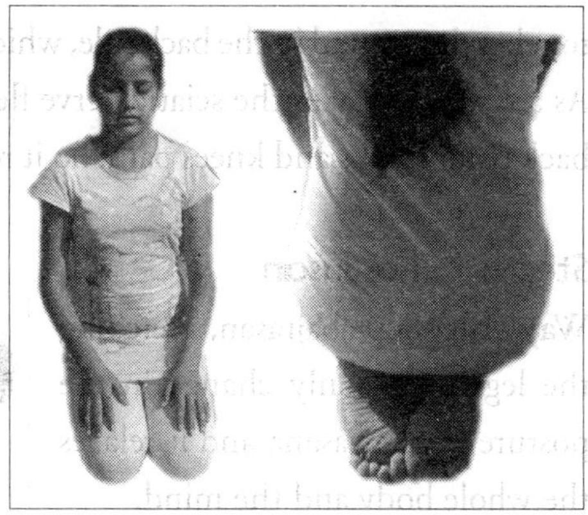

seconds. Then do again Jaanunaman or genuflection. Then come back in Bajrasan and relax 40 to 60 seconds.

Benefits Bajrasana is a very beneficial posture. It erects the spinal cord, which supports the neuro-function as well as glandular secretion required to maintain the harmony between body and mind.

It energises the digestive system and reduces gastric disturbances within the stomach and intestines. It supports hormonal secretion and maintains proper enzymization as well as proper secretion of bile from the gall bladder. As a result, the posture calms all the metabolic imbalances within the body and sooths mental distress also. Overall it strengthens the whole body and mind.

Step 7 Suptabajrasan

Way While sitting in Bajrasan, lie down so that the back of the head touches the ground and the back and spine should be arched.

Breathing Long and deep breaths should be taken.

Duration 15 to 30 seconds.

Benefits It is Supta-bajrasana or lying Bajrasana. The previous posture Bajrasana is a sitting posture. This posture relaxes the efferent and afferent nerves because before it, all the other postures were for bending and rushing blood to the head portion. Now, in this posture, all that pressures and tensions get released and normalcy prevails.

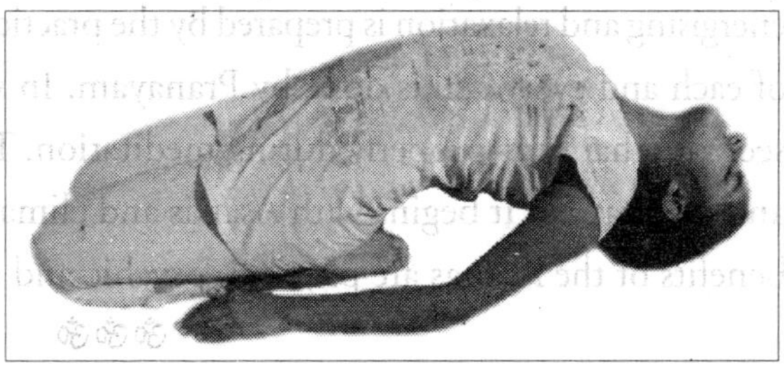

In this posture, the spine becomes arched and the head

touches the ground in the back side, which relaxes the back and the head portion. As a result, it makes the sciatic nerve flexible and helps avoid sciatic problems, back pain, thighs and knees pain. So it relaxes all the nerves from neck to knees.

Step 8 Shawasan

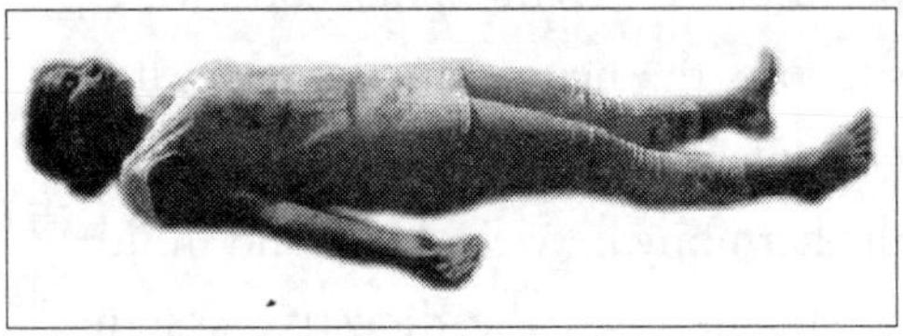

Way After Suptabajrasan, stretching the legs is the only change in the posture in Shawasana and it relaxes the whole body and the mind.

Benefits of Asanas

The benefits of Asanas are: Flexibility, stamination, psycho-somatic healing, the ground for pranayamic and meditative benefits.

Flexibility of the body is the main benefit of Asanas because the persons who do not practice Asanas find their bodies becoming very stiff. As a result, sciatic problems occur and all joints become very congested. The functioning of joints become dull and such an individual feels pain. A person becomes prone to strain and sprain. So, through regular practice of Asanas, flexibility of body is maintained.

Asanas stretch tense muscles, nerves and joints. At the same time all the obstacles and particles of toxic materials in the body are broken. As a result, blood circulates rapidly, giving stamina to all the organs of the body.

Psycho-somatic healing means establishing harmony within the body and mind to erase the basis of mental and physical ills. The ground for flexibility, energising and relaxation is prepared by the practice of Asanas and the purification of each and every cell is done by Pranayam. In sequential order, the harmonal secretion happens properly during meditation. This is the great benefit of yoga and meditation. It begins with Asanas and climaxes in meditation. Overall, the benefits of the Asanas are physical, psychic and spiritual healing.

ॐ ॐ ॐ

Five

Pranayam

Meaning and Motif of Pranayam

To answer the question what is the meaning of Pranayam, Maharshi Patanjali writes an aphorism in his treatise *Yoga Sutram*.

तस्मिनसति श्वासप्रश्वासर्योगतिविच्छेदः प्राणायामः

Tasminsati Shwasprashwasyorgativichchedah pranayamah.

This means having mastery over Asanas, the pause in the natural flow of breath is known as Pranayam.

The natural flow of breath is not Pranayam. To make an effort and stop breath is Pranayam. To stop the outgoing and incoming breaths in any way is Pranayam. For this reason, Patanjali says, "pause or change in normal speed of breathing is Pranayam".

The state of pause in breathing cannot be automatic. It is to be done deliberately. It is done effortfully. It is done by voluntary effort. This pause is known as a Kumbhak. In Pranayam, Kumbhak, the pause in breath is very important. It is not improper, if it is said that Kumbhak is the crux of Pranayam.

It is necessary to know all about Kumbhak, because it has been given so great importance in the context of the Pranayam. Pranayam is meaningless without a pause in breath or Kumbhak. So a voluntary and temporary deadlock or pause in natural breathing is Pranayam.

There are three phases in breathing. The breathing in or inhalation and breathing out, exhalation is a natural process of respiration. There is a little natural pause in between inhalation and exhalation. The three dimentions of breathing are given below:

1. Apurak (inhalation)
2. Rechak (exhalation)
3. Kumbhak (pause)

When we inhale the air from the atmosphere, that is called 'Apurak' (inhalation) and when we exhale the inhaled air to the atmosphere that is called rechak exhalation.In between inhalation and exhalation, there is a light pause that is called Kumbhak.

Phases of Kumbhak

Kumbhak is divided into three phases.

1. Antar Kumbhak (Inner pause)
2. Bahya Kumhak (Outer pause)
3. Keval Kumbhak (just pause)

Antar Kumbhak (Inner pause)

When after Apurak or inhalation, the inhaled air is stopped temporarily in the lungs, it is called Antar Kumbhak

Bahya Kumbhak (Outer pause)

After Rechak or exhalation, the air is stopped outside of the lungs that is called Bahya Kumbhak.

Keval Kumbhak

The stoppage of breath at any time–either while inhalation or exhalation–is called Kaval Kumbhak. Keval Kumbhak can be felt during the automatic process of respiration or sometimes when we get serious or shocking news, our breath stops by itself, without any effort. That is called Keval Kumbhk.

Charisma of Kumbhak

Kumbhak is an important phenomena in Pranayam. There is no meaning to Pranayam without Kumbhak. Especially the Bahya (Outer) Kumbhak, which has the capacity to push the energy upwards and helps attain miraculous power and clairvoyance.

This energy resides at the bottom of the spinal cord. When during our practice of Pranayam, Kumbhak makes all the air exhale out and at the same time, the navel portion becomes empty, a cavity is created. Through outer Kumbhak, this energy moves to fill the vacuum. When the energy reaches this point, in yogic terms it is called the Manipurak Chakra navel point. When the practitioner reaches this phase, he/she achieves a major step in the process of meditation.

Thus, Kumbhak is the governing point of the entire Pranayamic process.

Bandhas are complements of Kumbhak

Bandha means a 'lock' in a particular neuromuscular junction.

Due to contraction of a particular junction of nerves and muscles, a positive pressure is given in order to generate a viscero-receptive impulse. The run up of the energy within the body is stopped temporarily. And after some seconds, it is released.

Kumbhak means 'pause' of air within the body. The Bandhas are helpful in accomplishing the function of the Kumbhak. The Bandhas make the body mechanism support the benefits of Kumbhak. There are three main Bandhas or locks, which are given below.

1. Jalandhar Bandh (Chin lock)
2. Uddiyan Bandh (Belly lock)
3. Mula Bandh (Anal Lock)

Technique of Jalandhar Bandh

This is a chin lock. With errect spine, bending head touch the chest. Then Kumbhak gets support and promotion for the compression of air within the body.

Technique of Uddiyan Bandh

With errect spine, the whole abdomen is contracted tightly. This gives an acute support to the objective of Kumbhak. It is practised in sitting or standing position.

Technique of Mula Bandh

In sitting or standing position, the anal tract is contracted, applying force. Both the perineum and anal sphincters should be contracted in a synchronising manner.

Patanjali uses the word Gativichhed, for the deadlock or 'pause' in autonomous respiration, because that gives the perfect meaning of Pranayam.

The Kumbhak is effective only when the Bandhas play an effective role.. All the Bandhas should be applied during Kumbhak. If other Bandhas are difficult to applly, in the beginning only the Jalandhar Bandha should be applied while in Kumbhak, in order to compress, more and more fresh air within the body.

Without the Bandhas, specially the Jalandhar Bandha, Kumbhak must not be practised because the practise of Kumbhak may disturb and damage the natural functioning of the heart, lungs, liver etc. It can damage the nervous system, because of undue pressure and strain.

Motives of Pranayam

The first and foremost purpose of Pranayam is to control the stormy and whirlpooly mind. This is the main motif of Pranayam. As a side effect, decarbonization of each and every nerve and cell of the body takes place, along with the stilling of the vibrant and vagarent mind.

The pause or Kumbhak is an important factor of the entire gamut of Pranayam. Pranayam>pran + Ayam. Pran means the vital force or the life current which requires fresh air in the body in order to revive and servive the cells. Each and every cell requires fresh air to be properly active. Ayam means dimension. So Pranayam means the dimension of fresh air within the body. Dimension is not possible without Kumbhak.

Though fresh air is not the Pran but Pran requires fresh air. Fresh air is the conductivity of the Pran within the body. Without fresh air, no creature can live. So, generaly, the breaths are considered as Pran because of their importance for life. Normaly, a person takes 21,600 breaths within 24 hours. A man takes 15 breaths in a minute but this natural respiration is not Pranayam.

Through natural respiration, the exchange of maximum gases is not possible. So retention of breath is most important to oxygenate the body. The process of decarbonization takes place during the Kumbhak or pause.

Obviously, the exchange of oxygen and carbondixide across the thin walls of the alveoli and the blood capillaries take place more efficiently during the pause. In our body, metabolic function produces carbondioxide gas which is purified by blood in the heart and lungs. The more the Kumbhak, the more the purification of blood takes place.

When we inhale, we consume 20% oxygen and when we exhale, about 4% of this oxygen is retained for some seconds allowing uptake for the blood.

During Kumbhak, this percentage is increased to 8% to 10%. The metabolism gets more opportunity to use this oxygen as a result.

However, Pranayam's main objective is not oxygenation of blood but to cool and control the mind. Here it is necessary to know that Pranayam or breathing exercises are the techniques to still the mind.

It is our experience that whenever we become angry or emotionally upset, the rate, depth and way of our breathing increases. All the emotions and mental activities are related to the nervous system and aggravated mental activities affect our breaths. If we can control our breaths, we can control our life force, which is deeply connected with the mind.

The Pranayam controls the mind. The breathing exercises are the ways in which to calm down the mind. It is thus the objective of Pranayam to aquire a still mind and a purified body. The Pranayam heals us in the process of neurotherapy as well as psychotherapy. It develops our mind in such a way that we elevate ourselves in the path of meditation.

Fresh Air and Pranayama

Our automatic respiratory system inhales and exhales all the time 24x7. What enters into our lungs through the nostril during Pranayam?

Fresh air is an answer. Then there is another question, what is fresh air?

The atmosphere of our earth is a mixture of many gases in a proportionate quantum, such as nitrogen 78%, oxygen 20%, carbondioxide 0.03%, other noble gases 0.002%. Fresh air means all these gases in the atmosphere. We breath air and enliven ourselves. All creatures on earth breath this fresh air.

Why is it called oxygenation while the quantity of oxygen is only 20% of the total fresh air? Actually our body takes in the fresh air and absorbs only the oxygen. Rest of the air goes out in the process of auto-exhalation. As oxygen is only 20% in the fresh air, it is a compulsion of all creatures on this earth to take in fresh air from the atmosphere again and again, continuously, till death.

This is the process of breathing.

Our body is made of cells, it is nothing but a composition of cells. The cells require oxygen to be active and to accelerate the body mechanism. Just as in the atmosphere, there is a proportionate quantity of the gases, in the same way there is a proportionate quantum of all the ingredients of fresh air within our bodies.

So the measure of oxygen in the atmosphere is used in the process of Pranayama to increase the oxygen within the body because no oxygen means, no life. Our body requires oxygen, so that the Pran may be in conduction, and running throughout the body because this oxygen is conducive of Pran, life energy, or life current. Therefore, oxygenation is a must for the body. It is possible only through the inhalation of fresh air. Through Pranayamic techniques, the maximum amount of fresh air is supplied to the body and required proportion of oxygen is maintained.

Pranayam and Environment

Pranayama means oxygenation of the body. When oxygenation takes place in the body, the impurity of the blood is washed out. All the toxic materials in the blood, which reach within the body through food, water, air are cleaned out. These toxins are cleaned out by the techniques of Pranayama. It is called de-toxination. When detoxination takes place, gradually the purification of the nervous network also takes place and then alone, rejuvenation of the whole body takes place. This is a gradual achievement or the benefit of Pranayamic exercises.

If the environment is not in accordance with the norms and need of Pranayama, doing Pranayama may be harmful. Therefore, the environment,whether it is inside the room or outside the room, must be pure. The place where Pranayam is being practised must be full of fresh air. The entire environment must be full of fresh air.

Environments in big cities of the world are un-balanced or polluted, which disturb the proportion of oxygen, carbondioxide and nitrogen in the atmosphere.

This is pollution. We can depollute our rooms by lightening a wick of cow butter oil (cow ghee). Sages have said, a room can be purified as 10 gms of cow ghee, on burning, emits one ton of oxygen.

It is necessary to know what goes into our nostrils, which fulfills the requirement and purpose of Pranayama. Three things are necessary for our life. I. Air II. Water, and III. Food. We are very careful and cautious about the cleanliness and purity of food and water, but not about the air Air is the most important among these three. We cannot live without air even for a moment. Air is the most important requirement of the Pranayamic practice.

There are ways to depollute the room. Yag (or fire of sacrifice) to depollute the environment is a scriptural prescription. This is tradition. In many temples, a continuous burning of wicks dipped in cow ghee or any other natural edible oils is done with reverence. In Indian households, this is done as a devotional ritual, every morning and evening. In every inauguration, lightening of a wick is a ritual. The Rishic or scriptural prescription is behind all these ceremonies, associated with the purification of the environment.

Practice of Pranayama

There are so many kinds of Pranayam described in yogic scriptures but here only some important pranayamic exercises are being given.

The difference between common breathing and Pranayama is this: Pranayama is a scientific and systematic way of breathing to absorb more and more oxygen, to charge each and every cell of the body and mind.

1. Bhastrika

This is the composition of some spine-based light stretching exercises, inclusive of Pranayama and meditation. It is very effective and energetic.

Way Deep and full breathing in different stretched postures, seven in number.

Breathing 24 breaths in the 1st posture,

12 breaths in 2nd posture,

12 breaths in 3rd posture,

12 in 4th,

12 in 5th,

12 in 6th and

24 breaths in 7th posture.

Overall 108 breaths in one go. This is also known as Ajapa-japa. It is a breathing, chanting and a meditative exercise.

Note Six breaths may be used as a link for relaxation in between, as continuation.

Other Applied Tips of Bhastrika

A. Abdominal Breathing

Way This can be practiced while sitting or lying. Put your palms on your navel point. Sitting must be erect, upright.

Breathing Inhale deeply and let your belly expand and exhale and let it sink.

Duration To be repeated 12 times.

Concentration On the systole and diastole of the belly.

Benefits It strengthens the muscles of the diaphragm and provides scope for more oxygenation because the maximum amount of air from the body goes out and maximum fresh air comes into the lungs. It strengthens the lungs mechanism, protects children from asthmatic and breathing problems.

B. Chest Breathing

Way Inhale and expand the rib cage, exhale and contract the ribcage.

Duration 12 times. It is to be repeated.

Concentration On expansion and contraction of rib cage.

Benefits It strengthens the lungs and increases the dimension of lungs (absorption surface). It gives more scope for increasing oxygen absorption and enhances the capacity of the respiratory mechanism.

2. Kapal Bhati / Brain and Nasal cleaning

Way Sit in any meditative posture. Close your eyes. The spinal cord must be erect.

Breathing Exhale emphatically per second.

Duration At least 120 times.

Concentration On exhaling breath not inhaling.

Advanced Kapal Bhati

Way Everything is same only two exhales per

second are compulsory.

Duration Not less than 60, not more than 120 times. In begining acording to capacity.

Benefits There are so many benefits of this. All the jolts of exhaling air affect the whole navel portion. Kidneys, adrenal gland, prostate gland, Cowper's gland and the intestines. Overall, the glands and organs get energized. This protects from all major and minor diseases, whether heart or liver problems, kidney problem or cancer. It lightens the brain and helps avoids headache. It promotes cheerfulness, and erases nervousness and fragility of mind. It develops courage, caliber and confidence in children.

Precaution 120 breaths are the complete course for one time. One can practise less than 120 breaths in the beginning, add according to stamina and capacity and increase the number of breaths gradually.

3. Nadishodhan (Purification of the nervous network)

Nadi Shodan is a Sanskrit word. Nadi means nerves and Shodhan means purification. In this way Nadi Shodhan means the purification of the nervous system. The nerves, either afferent or efferent, and the veins and arteries which supply energy to every cell, are the communication channels to the brain.

In yogic scriptures, there are seventy two hundred million nerves. The poisonous materials that go into the body are removed by the Nadi Shodhan Pranayama.

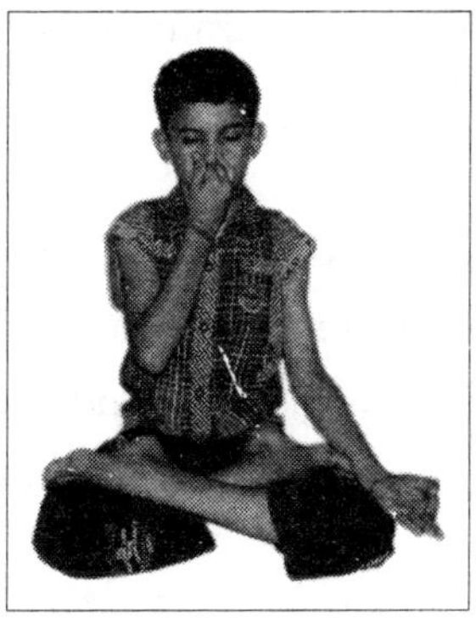

Sun Zone And Moon Zone–In yogic scriptures, the right nostril is called sun zone which regulates the heat within the body and the left nostril regulates the cooling within the body and is known as the moon zone. In this way, the body maintains its temperature of 98.4°C always. When the body needs heat, then it increases the temperature automatically. There are automatic heaters as well as coolers within the body. An air conditioner functions within the body.

The technique of Nadishodhan Pranayama activates the air conditioner within the body and escalates the flow of the life current. As an outcome, it energizes and rejuvenates the whole nervous system, which sharpens the mind and memory. It instils and stabilizes courage and confidence in the personality of children.

Suryabhedi / Sun activating

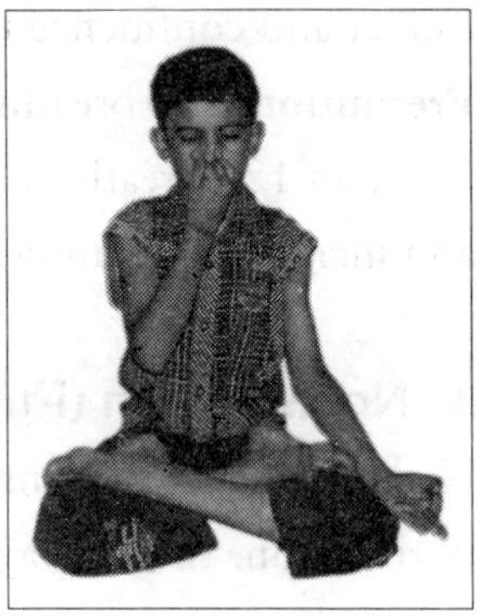

Way Sit in meditative posture in 'Padmasan'. Put the tip of thumb on right nostril. Keep index and middle finger on the bottom of thumb. It is called the pranav mudra. Afterwards, with the small and the ring finger on the left nostril, close the left nostril. Inhale through the right nostril and exhale through the left nostril.

Breathing Inhale through right nostril deeply and exhale through left nostril slowly.

Duration 12 times at least.

Concentration On incoming and outgoing breaths.

Chandrabhedi/ Moon activating

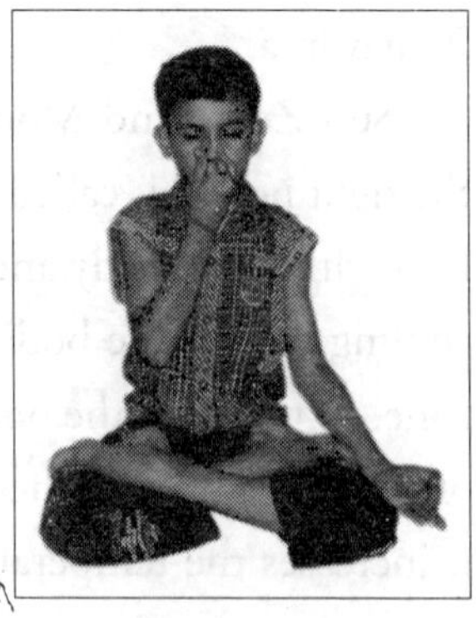

Way Everything is the same as above but now inhale through the left nostril and exhale through the right nostril.

Duration 12 times at least.

Benefits It escalests the heating and cooling procedure within the body and promotes purification of all the nerves of the body and mind.

Anulom and Vilom (Alternate nostril respiration)

Way All the conditions are the same as above but now inhale through the left nostril and exhale through the right nostril. And immediately, inhale through the right and exhale through the left nostril.

Breathing At least 24 breaths alternatively. Gradually increase number of breaths, according to stamina.

Concentration On incoming and outgoing breaths.

Antrang-Bahirang Kumbhak (Inner and outer retention)

Way Inhale through left nostril deeply and stop the breaths as long possible. Exhale through right nostril. Stop the breathing out as long as possible. Thereafter, inhale through right nostril and stop breathing out as long possible. Then exhale through lef nostrilt. Stop as long as possible. Repeat alternatively.

Caution While retaing of the breath, chin lock or jalandhar bandh is compulsory, otherwise it can harm the nervous system and mental mechanism.

Duration 24 breaths, one by one.

Note If any suffocation is felt, stop, pause for a while until the sense of suffocation eases. Gradually one's stamina will be increased.

Benefits of Nadi-shodhan Overall the collective effects of all the stages of Nadishodhan are to maintain the flow of life energy in an equal manner, within the Ida/moon nerve and Pingala/sun nerve. The body gets decarbonized and is richly oxygenated. The body and mind get great opportunity to be charged and energized. Each and every cell of the body and mind gets purified in this process.

Omayam

What is Om and what is Ayam? Patanjali writes [तस्य वाचक: प्रणव:] His name is Om. His means God's. Om is the name of God. It is supposed that Akash (sky) was created first, and then the vibration of Om started. Om is the first and the foremost sound. It is a sweet sound.

After a long time of meditation, this Om sound is heared in the body which gives the feeling of incessant, melodious tranquility. This is called Brahmanand or Shabd Brahma or Nadbrahm.

Om is the blend of four alphabets A+U+M+A+ which symbolize A or Lord Brahma , U > Symbolizes Lord Vishnu and M > symbolizes Lord Shiva. meaning creation, maintenance and distruction.

Two Ways of Omayam

1. Oral 2. Nasal

Oral Omayam

Way In the beginning, start practicing loudly. After good loud practice in murmuring, the last phase is mental only.

There are three ways of Omayam

1. O_ssssssssssssssssssssss_msss
2. O _ssssssssssssss_msssssssssssss.
3. O _ssssssssssssssssssssss_msssssssssss

Posture Padmasan or Ardhpadmasan, closed eyes, face relaxed.

Breathing Inhale and exhale through omayam.

Duration In the beginning 12 times, maximum 24 times.

Concentration On the Om sound's vibration.

Benefit The vibration of Om sound gives stamina to the nervous system of children. It improves the concentration of the kids. Alpha effect dominates the mind. Due to this alpha effect, blood pressure as well as heart rate is reduced. Galvanic skin resistance is increased. Depression and distress is minimized.

As many 24 chantings of the word Om in the morning and evening gives emotional stability, mental peace. It improves the memory of the kids as well as their IQ. The mind of the children become still. The Omayam gives the benefit of Pranayam and meditation too. Children feel cheerful and get mental stamina. It removes children's anger and fraustration. It is a para psychotherapy for children.

This is a perfect way of Sadhana , called the Prana Sadhana.

Nasal Omayam (Bhramari Pranayam)

Way Sit in padmasan, close the eyes and keep your spine errect. Keep mouth and jaws closed.

Breathing Inhale maximum amount of air possible and exhale, sounding Om nasaly.

Duration It last 12 times at most 24 times in one sitting.

Concentration On the Om sound's vibration.

Benefit Same as in oral Omayam but more effective than that.

Advanced Nasal Omayam (Bhramari Pranayam)

Way Everything is same only ears are to be closed here.

Sheetali Pranayam /Cooling breath

Way Sit in meditative posture. Expand your tongue and fold it to make a tube. Inhale slowly and deeply through the folded tongue. Stop the breath. After a short time, exhale through the nostrils.

Duration Practise at least 12 times.

Benefit It is a cooling Pranayama in summer. It quenches thirst. It multiplies the atoms of hydrogen within the body. It provides for flow of energy throughout the body. It purifies the blood.

Children suffering from pharyngitis and tonsilitis should not practice this yoga. Also if their throat is sensitive. It is useful only in summer.

Sheetakari Pranayam

Way It is very similar to Sheetali. The tongue must be turned towards the backside. The tip of the tongue should touch the palate.

Breathing Inhale through the teeth and the tongue. Close the mouth and normalize the tongue. Stop the breath for at least 6 seconds. Then exhale through the nostrils.

Duration Repeat it 12 times.

Benefits Same as sheetali

Benefits of Pranayam

Pranayam erases the scope of all types of diseases. Pranayam protects from contagious disease. Pranayam strengthens the immunity of a person. The practitioner of Pranayam acquires good resistance power and remains disease free throughout his/her life. Pranayamic techniques energise the life current and that energises the vital force, providing a safeguard all around the practitioner.

Through the practice of yoga and Pranayam, the possibilities of cancerous diseases are also removed. Pranayam purifies the blood, absolutely essential to the functioning of the body mechanism. This blood is nothing but the composition of RBCs, WBCs and thrombocytes. Approximately 5 liters of blood circulates in the human body.

Each cubic mm of blood contains 5 million RBC (red blood cells). The cells contain protien, iron, haemoglobin which are quickly bound with oxygen. It also contains an enzyme which is called carbonic anhydrase. This enzyme facilitates the release of carbondioxide. Average life of RBC is about 120 days. The degeneration of the cell happens in the liver, spleen, bone marrow and lymph nodes. The haemoglobin is changed into bilirubin, which is released into the blood. The liver cells take this matter from the blood and add to the bile. New RBCs are produced in the bone marrow. In this way, RBCs help in exchanging carbondioxide of the body with the oxygen of the atmosphere. The above mechanical and chemical functions get energy and the healing of the body accelerates.

In the same way 7000 WBCs are found in one cubic mm of blood. WBCs kill all the harmful bacterias and foriegn organic particles. This defence mechanism is related with our immunity system which works against infectious diseases. Therefore, the process of practice of Pranayam is very effective. If the defence mechanism is dull and slow, then blood cancer and other diseases happen.

Thrombocytes are 250,000 in number in one cubic mm of blood. They help in the process of blood clotting, in case of injury. All the antibodies are here, which play a protective role against various bacterias, virus, toxic materials. Through the practice of yoga and Pranayam ,this process has revolutionized. The practice of Pranayam makes the practitioner free from every disease.

If the body is totally purified there is no scope of any disease and it is possible only through the practice of Pranayam. The regular practice of yoga and Pranayam gives a feel of happyness, a satisfaction and a calm and cool state of mind all the time. Tension or stress are never felt. Yoga and Pranayam maintain homeostasis. The practitioner is free from psychosomatic diseases like asthma, diabetes, arthritis. The special feature of the practice of yoga and Pranayam is that the glandular system of the female finds greater benefit than the male practitioner. We know that the hormonal balance results in the balance of mind and body, which can be acquired by the practice of yoga and Pranayam, meditatively.

With the practice of Kapalbhati, oxygen absorption is increased 10% to 40 percent, while in normal breathing it is only 4%. In this way, a big quantity of carbondioxide is washed out from the blood. In normal breathing, the intake of fresh air is 7.5 litre per minute, but while practising Kapalbhati, as much as 20.5 litres per minute can be taken in. Almost three times more oxygenation takes place than in normal breathing.

Pranayama is therefore an acute way for purification of the body and stilling the mind.

ॐ ॐ ॐ

Six
Meditation

Meaning and Motif of Meditation

Meditation is a completly scientific way to heal the human body. Only human body has the capacity, scope and privilege to practise it, because controlled mind is the source of good health and the gateway to God.

Meditation is the way to mind control. The mind is very powerful and vagrant. When it is concentrated on one point, it gives tremendous results.

A yogi concentrates on God and knows all about God and the secrets of the universe. Scientists concentrate and makes inventions. Artists concentrate on art and achieve a lot. In the same way, students concentrate on their studies and obtain good results and career.

First, let us scan the word meditation. This originated from the Latin word

'Meditari'. This meditari word originated from the etym 'Medere' of the Latin language that means 'to heal'. Meditation is, therefore, the science of healing. This science of healing is at the physical, psychic and spiritual levels in case of yoga. So meditation is medication for the body.

We know that our body has an autonomous, natural, medicative system which is active every now and then to harmonize visceral metabolic organs. Through meditation, a supportive ground gets opened, to channelize the inner auto- function of healing within the body. It helps level the vital force, maintenance of hormonal balance, potentization of neural strength, escalates glandular activation and the digestive system etc.

Scriptural Definition of Meditation

Maharshi Patanjali defines meditationas = तत्र प्रत्ययैकातनता ध्यानम्

(Tatra pratyayaikatanata dhyanam) which means continuous concentration on one subject. Continuous concentration without interruption is meditation.

Another definition is given by Maharshi Vedvyas ध्यानं निर्विषयं मनः (Dhyanam nirvishayam manah)] which means, a subjectless mind is the state of meditation. A mind where there is no agitation is meditation, or the state of 'no mind' is meditation.

When the meditator attains such a state of trance through the practice of meditative exercises, something transcendental happens. While the practioner becomes calm, all his/her stimulating senses are quietend. Then God's thoughts flow through meditator's mind and the meditator speaks like God, acts like God, loves like God with everyone. The process of enlightenment starts on such a ground.

First the mind power is concentrated on one point. In course of time the mindstuff is emptied of thought imprints. In such a thoughtless state of mind, some or the other miracles happen. The first definition is for the beginers, and the second is for the little advanced practitioners.

Four Postures for Meditation

1. Spinal posture
2. Finger posture
3. Tongue posture
4. Eye posture

Lord Krishna's instruction for sitting in meditation were:

समं काय शिरोग्रीवं धारयनाचलम स्थिर: ।
सम्प्रेक्ष्य नासिकाग्रं स्वं दिशश्चनावलोकयन।।

Samam Kaya shirogreevam dharayanachalam sthirah.
Samprekshya nasikagram swam dishashchanavalokayan.

This means, with head, body and neck errect, stay in this position without stirring or moving, concentrating on the middle point between the eyebrows. Do not look hither and thither.

Spinal Posture

The spinal posture must be right. The spine should be errect, in order to facilitate relaxation of all the visceral organs. All the internal organs get free from pressure. The figure in the previous page clarifies how glandular secretion is managed by the spine. The spine is the source of all the functions and activities of all the inner organs of the body. Bending the spine is very harmful. It is for this reason that yoga always prescribes that one must sit erect always to maintain the flow of energy into every cell and organ of the body.Sucha posture allows free flow of energy that gives the enthusiasm for study and mental work.

Finger Postures (Jnan mudras)

Finger postures are very important. These have a vital role in meditation. It is popularly called jnan mudra. The mudras enhance mental function of children. Three Jnanmudras are given below.

Jnanmudra I

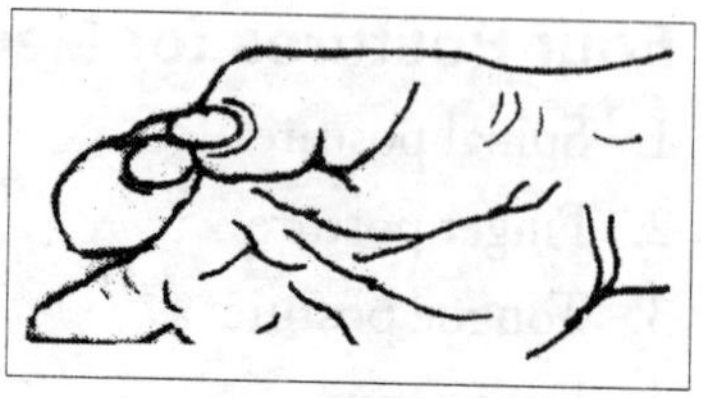

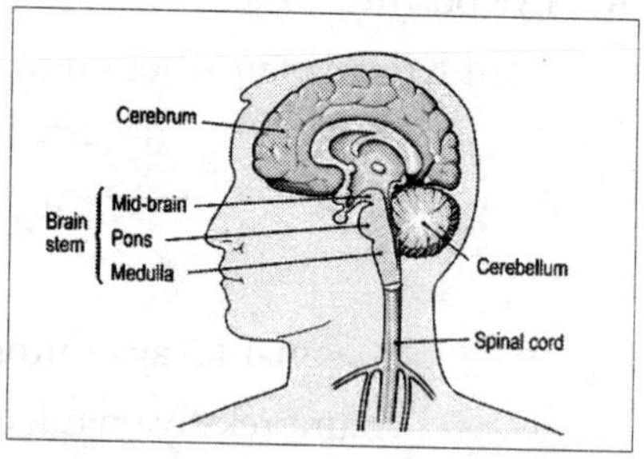

This is the first step of jnanmudra. It acupresses the point of the cerebrum, which is a major part of for the integral mechanism of the brain. Through this jnanmudra, the the whole cerebrum gets activated and energised. This organ is also known as 'big brain'. This big brain is just like a super computer. It is the recorder of all knowledges and informations which are acquired thrrough the five senses– eyes, ear, nose, tongue, and skin. This big brain is energised through Jnanmudra I. The inactivated part of the cerebrum is activated and helps in maximum utilization of the mind, helping mental efficiency. Mental power gets enhanced through this Jnanmudra.

Jnanmudra II

This second step of Jnanmudra acupresses the point of the mid brain, the pituitary gland. This pituitary gland contains many hormones.

It governs all the functions and activities within the body. The hormones are responsible for the functioning of the whole body. Pituitary gland is the source of health and harmony in children.

It also controls the optic nerve. In this way, the eye is protected through meditation. This gland secretes hormones which are responsible for balanced development of the body. If these are not secreted properly, then the height and balanced growth of the child is hindered and the child developes into a dull boy or girl. Meditation promotes the secretions which helps gain good height and sharp mind. It is the somatotropic hormone which is very important.

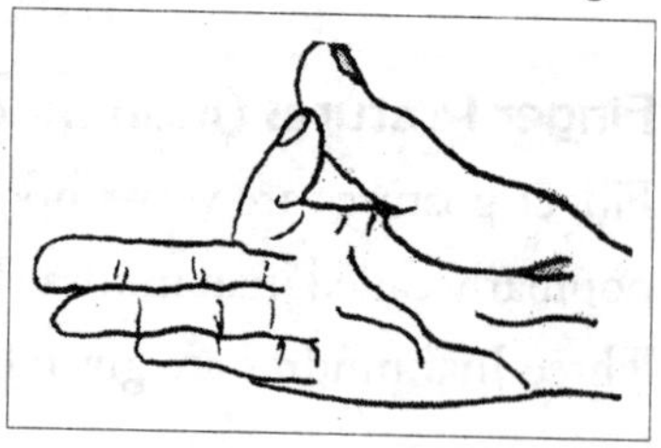

Another hormone called the thyrotrophic hormone balances calcium and other minerals within the body. This is also secreted by the pituitary gland. If it is not secreted properly or this function is inactive, then obesity and arthritis affect the tender body of children.

Still another hormone, named the ATC hormone, helps reduce the cause of diseases of the heart, kydney, liver, lungs. It cures allergy. It maintains the health of inner organs.

There is another hormone which is responsible for development of the ova and the graffian follicles in the ovary and the sperms in the testis. Proper secretion of this hormone makes children grow into a complete male or female. If the secretion is not proper, then the child may grow into an impotent and sterile man or woman. If a five-year-old child is taught to meditate at least for twelve minutes, he or she is free from such problems. FSH and LH hormones are responsible for this and meditation helps in proper secretion of these hormones.

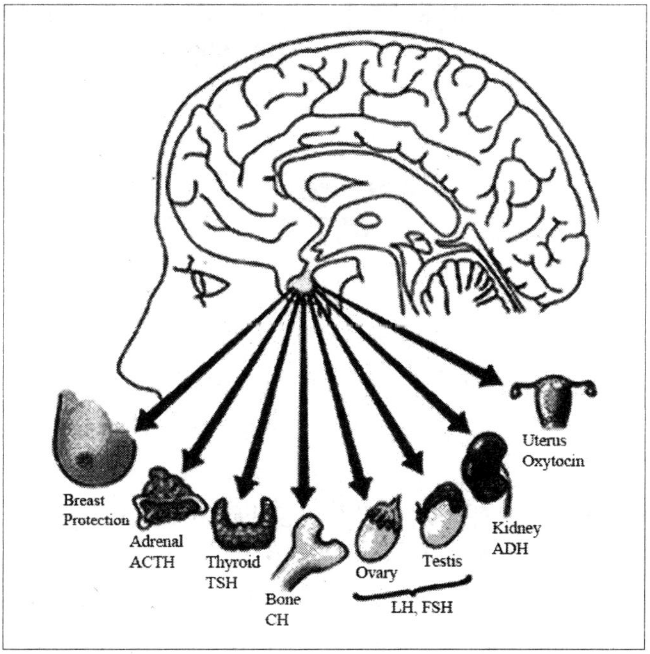

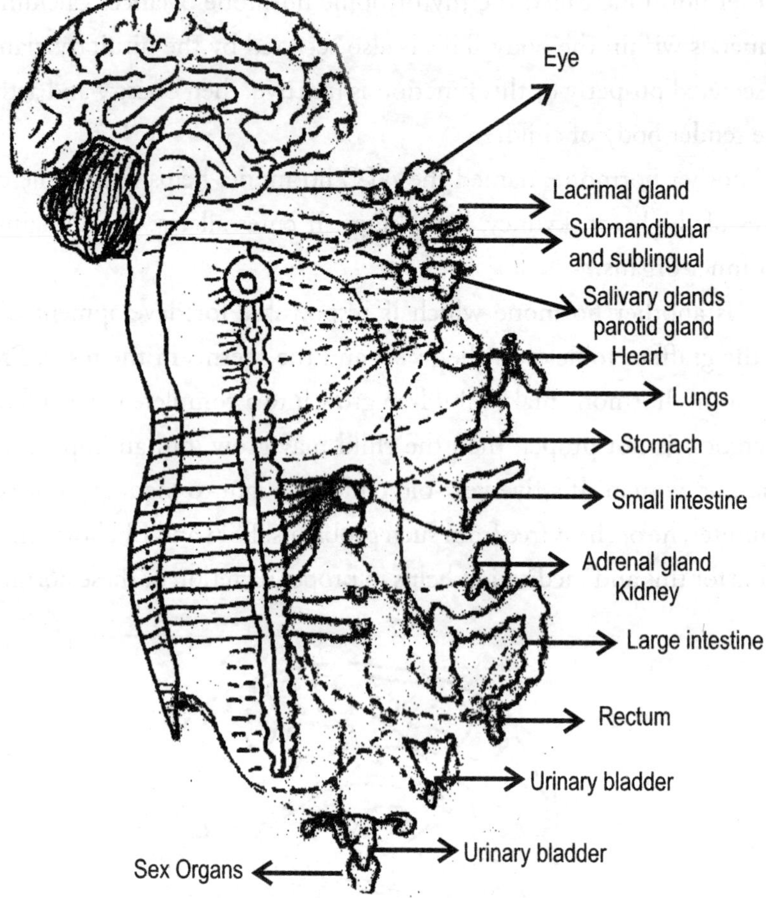

Pituitary Gland and function and
its effects over other glands and organs of the whole body.

For Easy Childbirth

Another hormone is also secreted by this gland, which is responsible for easy child birth, without much pain. This gland gets gets partly inactive, when a woman does not meditate. Oxytocin is the hormone responsible for proper delivery without pain and surgery. The posture of meditation prepares the ground for hormonal secretions. The Jnanmudra activates the glands and their proper functions.

To protect the whole body and the mind, nature has given all the medicine within the body in the form of hormones responsible for good health. To sit in meditation is the only way to activate all the glandular function and the body mechanism. Therefore, yoga and meditation are very good for children.

When any old man or woman wants to meditate, he/she will require one to three hours to enjoy the same benefits but children get the same benefit within 24 minutes.

In this manner, we can know that meditation is medication. Any child can benefit from meditation within 24 minutes. This is the most important Jnanmudra of all the Jnanmudras. So regular meditation is very necessary for every child to be healthy, happy, and sharpminded.

Jnanmudra III

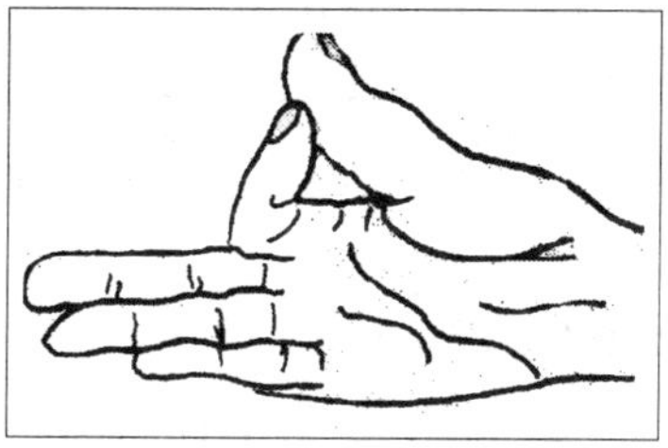

It acupresses the pineal gland's point. The pineal gland is responsible for secreting the hormone melatonine, which is responsible for mental maturity and calm state of mind. This is the ground for realization. When the ground is laid through incessant and assiduous meditation, then a time comes when something comes out from the glands and gives the benefit of meditation. Realization is also the result of hormone-secretion. Therefore, the Jnanmudra III is very important for the realization of the ultimate reality.

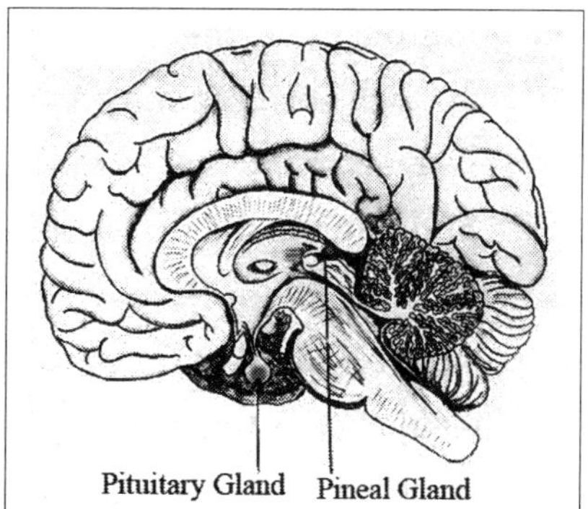

IV Final Relaxing Posture (Vitraag Mudra)

It is the last and final phase of meditation that energises again the cerebrum, pituitary and pineal glands, all together to make the mental-mechainsm strong. This is to help children learn their lessons and lessen their lethargy. This Jnanmudra can be seen in the pictures and idols of Lord Mahavir Jain and Buddha. It is called the Vitraag posture.

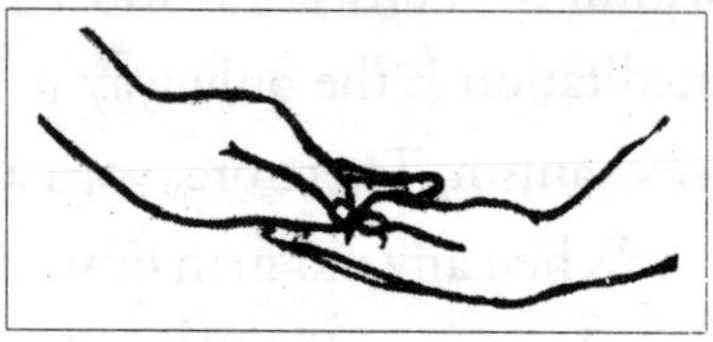

Tongue Posture

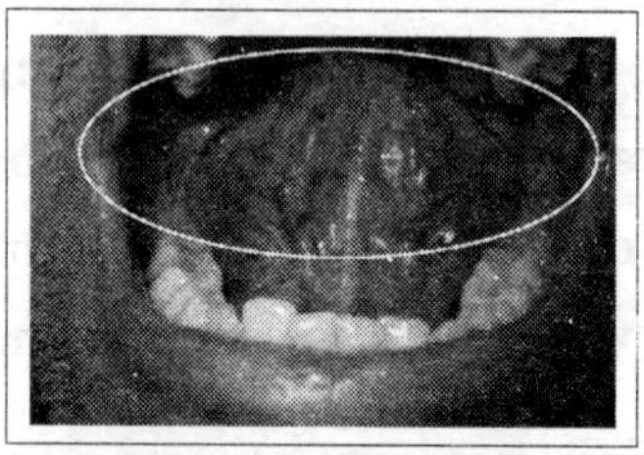

It is a very important posture. In this posture, the tongue takes the U shape, towards the palate part of the mouth. The tongue turns towards the palate. It is called Khechari mudra or nabhomudra in yogic terms.

This mudra helps to elevate the vital force upwards, so essential to achieve the benefits of meditation. It stimulates the facial muscles. It provides a complexion. It removes nervousness from the entire face and personality.

Eye Posture

Eye posture is with the eyes closed. The concentration is on the third eye, between the two eyebrows. The eyes and the tips of the index finger always emit energy. The index fingers take a U turn and touches the tips of thumbs, which are the points for cerebrum, major part of the brain and also the center of cosmic energy.

When the index finger touches the thumb, the brain gets charged because the cosmic and individual energy start to merge into one cycle, in one circuit. Eye posture, finger posture and the spinal cord start becoming erect, and they charge the batteries of the body. Just like the charging of a mobile phone's battery. Children sit in meditation and charge their body batteries themselves, regularly. In this manner, children can remain free from illnesses all their lives.

Dharana, Dhyan and Samadhi

(Concentration, Meditation and Trance)

Samadhi or trance is nothing but the fructification of the long-time practice of meditation. Meditation is a super conscious state of mind. It is the absorption of the egoistic self. It is the dilution of the being into the super being, it is the state of realization, where mere spirit vibrates. Only one entity is realized. There are two types of Samadhi.

1. Savikalpak 2. Nirvikalpak

Savikalpak Samadhi

In the Savikalpak Samadhi, the see-er sees the seen, along with the self. There is only partial inhibition of the mind. The realization of oneness and wholeness, or the realization of the existence of individuality within the totality occurs. Aham Brahmasmi means there is one reality and I am within that. I am the part and parcel of that. There is no difference of this or that.Self and the Other.

Nirvikalpak Samadhi

In Nirvikalpak Samadhi the see-er and the seen both are unified. Only one existence is vibrated and nothing else.

This is the condition of complete awareness. In such a state ,the meditator sees without eyes, tastes without tongue, hears without ears, smells without nose, touches without skin.

There is complete dis-function of the thought waves. It is the state of 'no mind', full absorption of the thinking process. Just as one drop of water merges into the ocean and then there is no drop but only the ocean. Just like a sea without waves. It is called Samadhi in the scriptures which is the culmination of the incessant and assiduous practice of meditation.

Practice of Meditation

Tip I Dhyan (Meditation)

Way Sitting in Padmasan

Breathing Normal

Duration 12 minutes to 24 minutes

Concentration On the pumping and pressing of all the critical points one by one.

Concentration Between the two eyebrows.

Final Touch Rub the palms and put over the eyes. Massage the whole face, eyes, head, ears, cheeks, the whole neck and the throat portion.

Tip II Jap (Chanting)

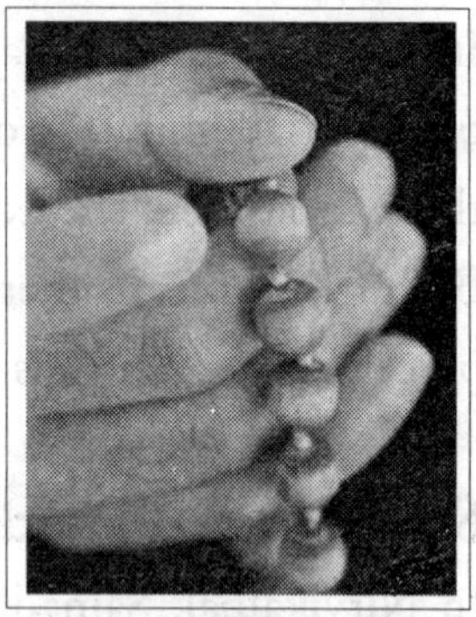

Way Sit in Padmasana or Ardhapadmasana. Take the Mala (chanting beads), and chant the Mantra you prefer. Gayatri Mantra is the best Mantra for children. This Mantra was given to children during initiation when they joined Gurukul or school. The Mantra empowers children and elevates them to higher levels of spirituality and sharpens their intellect.

Tip III Tratak (Gazing)

Tratak means to gaze at one point. Tratak is a way of meditation. It satisfies the terms and conditions of meditation. Two kinds of tratak are described in the scriptures. 1. Antarang, 2. Bahirang

1. Antarang / Inner Gazing

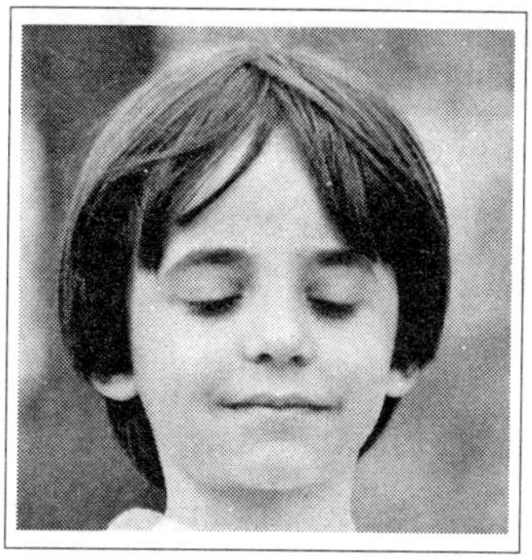

This inner gazing process begins after closing the eyes. To concentrate on the middle point of eyebrows is the inner tratak. The meditator concentrates his/her attention to the middle point of the eyebrows, to the third eye.

2. Bahirang / External gazing

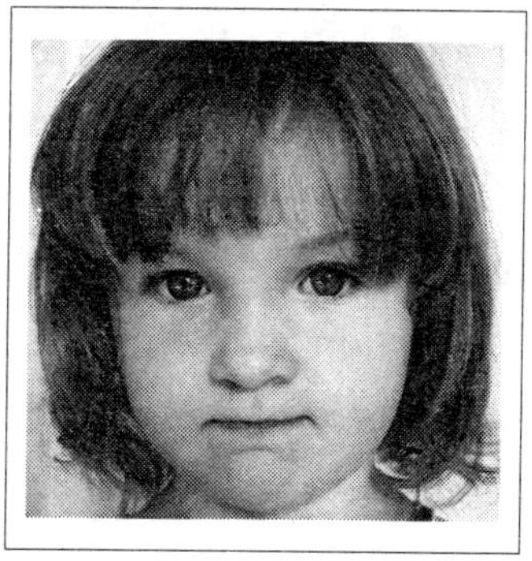

It is gazing outward. The concentration is on any point, with open eyes, continuously. It may be candle/ wick, flame, tree, idol in temple etc.

Way Sit in meditative posture. Look at the flame continuously. Gaze on the flame of a candle or a wick without closing the eyes. Relax and start again. In this way, both the inner and outward tratak may be applied one by one. As long as possible, do tratak with open eyes, otherwise close the eyes. Suppose that you are gazing at a candle flame. First you gaze ta the flame, it is outer tratak and then close your eyes and gaze at the flame. It becomes inner tratak.

Duration Start with 12 minutes, later allot more minutes.

Benefit It provides visual stamina and concentrative power to children.

Benefits of Meditation

Meditation is a healing science as the word's etymological meaning clarifies. It is just like a neurotonic. It strengthens the sensitivity and awareness. It maintains hormonal balance. It develops intuition and clairvoyance. When anyone meditates, the divine energy flows over and around the meditator. This state soothes the turbulent and maddening senses and mind.

The meditation also helps develop an ideal level of courage and caliber in the personality of the meditator. It develops capacity, patience, vigilance, intelligence, diligence, peace and love in the meditators. It makes the man/woman positively complete. It erases all the negative thinking. It removes hopelessness as well as nervousness from the personality.

Meditation means treatment at three levels–the physiological, psychological and spiritual. After long practice of meditation, the meditator gets to realize the ultimate reality and the secret of all the secrets. The meditator is able to reveal the mystery of the mysterious universe, cosmos. In a higher stage of the practice of yoga and meditation, something divine happens, beyond this material world which is known as transcendental.

Recent Researches and Benefits

Meditation is not the research of ancient sages only, but even today many scientists are keen and interested in experiments that validate yoga and the benefits of meditation. Some experiments and the conclusions are mentioned below.

Researchers R K Valance and Herbert Benson experimented for a long time and concluded that during meditation, oxygen's use reduces. Within five minutes time duration, the consumption of oxygen gets reduced by 20%. It means, while for the activation of the body mechanism much more oxygen is consumed, when anyone sits for meditation, oxygen and energy are saved. This saved oxygen and energy start rejuvenation of each and every cell of the body and mind, and provides great relaxation.

Paramhans Yogananad had long ago written, "Kriyayoga is simple physio-psychological method by which human blood is decarbonised, and recharged with oxygen. The atoms of this extra oxygen are transmuted into life current to rejuvenate the brain and spinal centers. By stopping the accumulation of venomous blood, the yogi is able to lessen or prevent the decay of tissues. The advanced yogi transmutes his cells into energy.

When the person sleeps, the galvanised skin resistance increases 100% to 200% while in meditation, the galvanised skin resistance increases 250% to 5000% , which provides very deep relaxation."

One American scientist says that through meditation, a person who is a drug or alcohol addict can easily be free from them.

The British Journal of Psychology notes an experiment on twenty person, in which a researcher gave them a Mantra to chant and made them sit for meditation. After one month, he found a tremendous change in their behavior, temperament and nature. In the beginning all the participants were very uneasy, unquiet and depressed but at last, they became very calm and cool.

As we know through Jnanmudras, the pitiutary and pineal glands are stimulated to secrete the harmones properly. The newly discovered harmone, melatonin, is very important for our mental well being. The lack of this harmone aggravates anger and tension. A person becomes very arrogent and foulmouthed, very nervous and impatient. The parent compound of melatonin harmone is serotonin. This serotonin harmone is made from the amino acid tryptophan. Melatonin is secreted from the pineal gland. During the day, the pineal gland produces high levels of serotonin and at night produces melatonin. If such secretion is stopped or disturbed, a person can get frustrated and become a victim of dementia.

Proper secretion of melatonin is possible only during meditation. So, through meditation, not only this harmone but all the other harmones we have discussed, are secreted which give a sense of well being to the individual. Melatonin, especially, gives a calming feeling of happiness in the psyche of the individual.

Recent researches reveal some more wonderfull facts. During meditation, the brain emanates the alpha waves. Sometimes the Theta and Delta waves too. When the mind is cool and the brain is calm, the Alpha waves radiate. When the mind is possessed of tension, depression, or excitement the theta and delta waves emanate.

The brain is nothing but a big electrical circuit which always sends messages back and forth, between different points and centres of the brain. Actually, the brain generates a small amount of electricity known by the use of a machine called electroencephalogram. The waves are the same but according to vibration or frequency they are named alpha, beta, theta and delta etc. Alpha waves cycle 7 to 13 vibrations per second. Theta, delta and beta are of 13 to 30 vibrations per second, opposite to the alpha effect. These cause tension, depression, outbursts of temper, anger and anxiety.

The discovery of Alpha waves and their effect over the physique and psyche gave scientists an opportunity to develop a bio-feedback system. This bio-feedback system is a method by which, artificially, the body can get the benefit of the alpha waves from a machine. EEG is used to diagnose diseases like epilepsy, neuro and brain damage. Experts know how to stimulate or inject activity in the brain. Medical experts estimate that the human brain has 100,000,000,000,000 cells. Whatever we think and feel, that is nothing but the electrochemical activity within brain cells. Even now research and experiments are going on to learn of the nature and responses of the brain. Some recent research done in Los Angeles says yoga also helps the immune system to fight the AIDS virus.

ॐ ॐ ॐ

SEVEN

HASAYAM (LAUGHTER THERAPY)

Meaning and Motif of Hasayam

Just as natural flow of respiration is not Pranayam, in the same way, natural laughter is also not Hasayam yoga.

When one pauses deliberately in breathing, then the breath is known as Pranayam. Then, and then only, it gives the benfits of Pranayam. In the same way, when laughter is exercised as a Pranayam, then it is a Hasayam. Otherwise, it is nothing more than laughing and breathing.

When the breathing is done technically, then it becomes Pranayam. When one laughs according to set rules, technically, then it becomes a yoga, full of Pranayamic benefits. Then it becomes Hasayam yoga, a complete laughter therapy. A complete, preventive therapy.

Hasayam is a completely scientific process of laughing, which gives benefit to practitioners not only at the physical and psychic level but also at the spiritual levels.

When a person is happy, he likes to laugh and when he laughs it means he is happy. Laughing is an expression of happyness. Laughter and happyness are synonymous with eachother. All the characteristics of Pranayam are present in the Hasayam yoga. Apurak, Kumbhak and Rechak (inhalation, pause, exhalation) continue over the entire Hasayam process. The vibration of laughter gives great potency to Hasayam and then it becomes more useful and beneficial than Pranayam.

Hasayam is nothing but a scientific technique which gives power and potency to the practitioner.

Don't worry, be happy. Laughing is a very good exercise for health. Anyone who feels happy, laughs. When someone feels unhappy, he/she does not laugh. If some one laughs, there is no scope of unhappiness. Laughing is a natural and energetic activation of the body mechanism. When some one laughs, his whole body vibrates. This vibration gives impetus to the flow of energy within the body. This thrust creats storms and whirlpools of energy to flow and the person falls, runs, sits, lies down while laughing. The person enjoys the ecstasy of sensation through laughing.

Very few people know that laughter is a therapy when it is enjoyed scientifically. Only human beings have the privilege of laughing. No other being can laugh. Hasayam is the need of today's tense and sad people.

Meditative Values of Laughter

The human psyche is a mixture of three substances–mind, intellect and ego. The purpose of yoga and meditation is to rationalize the psyche of the person. Laughter helps in this rationalization.

According to yogic scriptures, mind is very vibrant and vagrant. It is very difficult to control. The psyche is the arena of mind, intellect and ego. When ego dominates the psyche, the humans act arrogant, wild. When mind dominates, humans are infatuated and attached to worldly matters. When the intellect dominates the psyche, humans act very calm and cool. This state of psyche is required always by all. The fluctuations of the mind, ego and intellect go on. Competition for domination continues always.

It is absolutely necessary to dominate the psyche with intellect. It requires a continuous effort to be an intellect-dominated person. In this, laughter is very efficacious. It is a very psychotherapeutic way to dominate the intellect over the psyche.

Though the laughter exercise is done by the domination of the mind, but after the final touch, the mind becomes still and the intellect gets an opportunity to dominate. This domination gives the practitioner a stand- still mind, sharp intelligence and an acute sense of humour. It gives the practitioner a positive approach, full confidence and caliber. This state is compulsory for meditative benefits.

The meditative effect of laughter is that a vibrant and vagrant mind, which is not fit for meditation, becomes calm and still through laughter.

The Physiology of Laughter

While laughing, one's belly gets agitated and through the movement in the navel portion, the centre of the nervous nucleus is activated. The flow of blood increases and infuses the whole body. Each and every nerve and cell is energized and rejuvenated. The face is filled with reddish blood. Thus, the face becomes rosy after laughter. Adrenal glands get activated.

There are two adrenal glands. These are located near both the kidneys. These glands maintain the discipline of the heart, liver, lungs, kidneys and the factory of insuline-producing islets of Langerhans which is responsible for supply of energy all over the physique. It supplies energy into each and every cell of the body. All the tissues and glands get activated and maintain proper functions

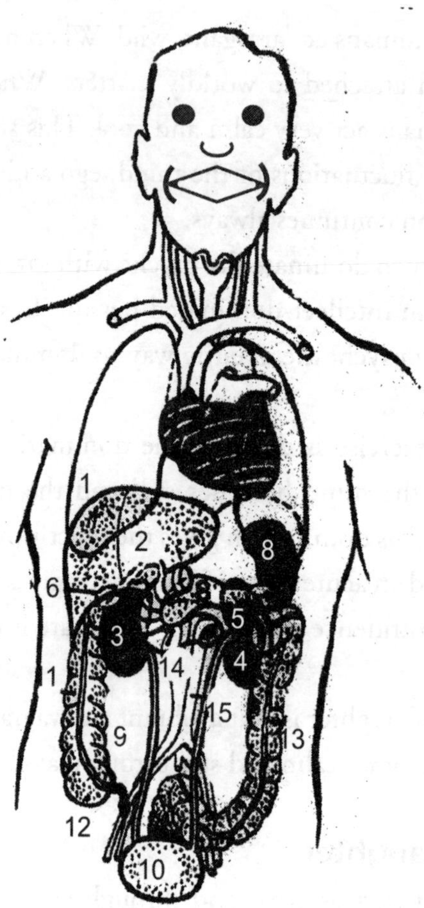

1. Heart
2. Liver
3. Right Kidney
4. Left Kidney
5. Spleen
6. Gallbladder
7. Duodenum
8. Pancreas
9. Urator
10. Urinary bladder
11. Ascending colon
12. Appendix
13. Descending colon
14. Inferior vena cava
15. Aorta

of the body mechanism. Overall this laughter protects from diabetes, heart problems, acidity, obesity and such other illnesses.

Yogic Facts of Laughter

Laughter is based on vowels of the Sanskrit language A,I,U,E,O, AM. The laughter of a person is based on any one of vowels given above. Some one laughs ha ha ha –the A tone. Some one laughs, hi hi hi. Some one laughs hu hu hu. Someone laughs he he he. Someone laughs ho ho ho. When anyone chuckles–it

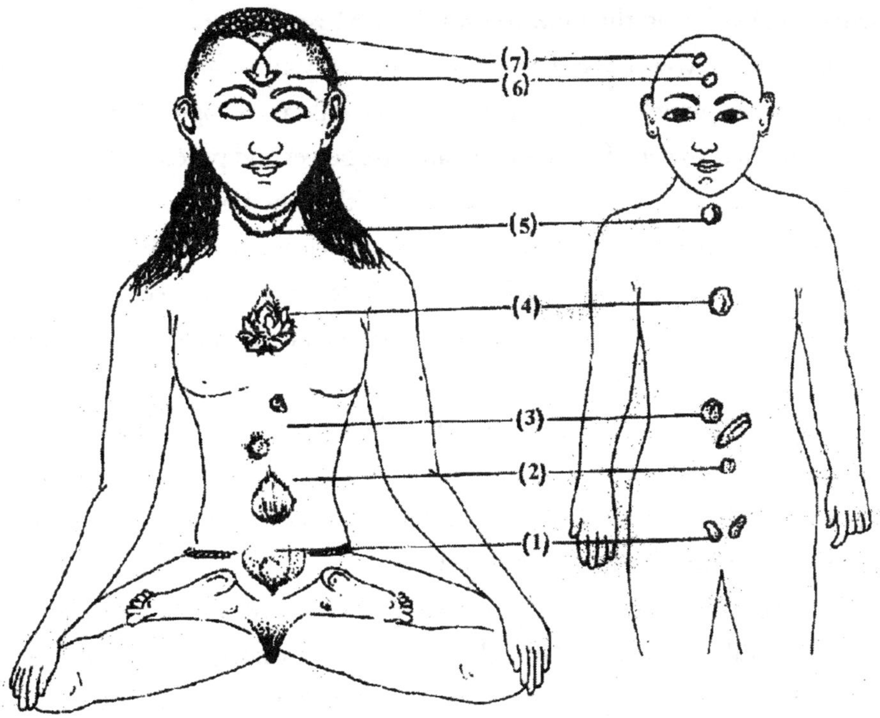

Chart of Connectivity with Chakras

Glands	Chakras	No.	Vowels	Pronunciations	Keywords	
Pineal, cerebrospinal fluid	Sahasrar	7	AM	Umpire	Om	ॐ
Pituitary, brain power	Ajnachakra	6	O	Om	Om	ॐ
Thyroid/parathyroid, Lungs body temperature.	Vishudhi	5	O	Om	Ham	हं
Thymus and pancreas, child growth	Anahat	4	E	Eight	Yam	यं
Adrenal, pancreas	Mainpurak	3	U	too	ram	रं
Solar plexus and navel Portion	Swadhisthan	2	I	He	vam	वं
Sex, testicles, prostate couper	Muladhar	1	A	audit	lam	लं

means, laughs closing the mouth–then the AM vowel is applied.

All the above vowels are connected with the mystic points of potency within the spinal cord, which are popularly known Chakras in yogic science.

A particular vowel effects and activates the power and potency of a particular Chakra. Laughter generates a lot of energy within the body and flows through the nervous network. The body fluctuates to congenialize the conductivity of electricity generated through laughter. The energy produced by laughter is controlled and concentrated by these vowels towards a particular potency of mystic point, or the Chakras.

The chart given on the page clearifies the connectivity of Chakras, glands, vowels and keywords or Beej Mantras and the effects of practice of laughter.

Overall, the climax of yoga is achieved in the state of Satva, or in the domination of intellect over mindstuff.

So, through laughter, such ground is prepared and maintained easily. The transcendental state is very difficult to attain. But through laughter, it is very easy. In the first phase, it protects from all the bodily ills and in the second phase all the mental ills and in third phase, it cures all the spiritual ills. First phase is practised with loud laugh, the second phase with silent laughter and in the third phase, only the memory of the first and second phases, without laughing. This laughter is a complete therapy.

Practice of Hasayam

Phase I

Way All the vowels are to be used one by one. from A to Am.

Posture Sitting in meditative position, with finger posture Jnanmudra. There should not be any movement in the body. It is advised to sit quite errect with closed eyes.

Breathing Exhale all the air from the lungs and inhale fresh air. Laugh exhaling the breath. Repeat it thrice. While exhaling, shrink your belly or navel portion.

Ist Step – Exhale out

IInd Step – Inhale in

IIIrd Step – Laugh

IVth Step – Relax. Breath with gap. Then breathe again. Repeat I to III.

Concentration on laughter vowels: A,I,U,E,O, AM, one by one all the vowels.

Anulom and Vilom of Laughter

In this Hasayam or laughter exercise, all the vowels are to be covered within a single inhaled breath. This step is final to step I of phase I.

Way

I Step – exhale out

II Step – inhale in

III Step – laugh in all the vowels A, I, U, E, O, AM sequentialy, within one exhaling breath, it means all the vowels are to be covered within a single exhaling breath. This is Anulom and in Vilom, it is the reverse. Anulom starts from A to Am but in Vilom it is to be started from AM and on to A.

This laughing exercise is the most concentrative. It improves concentration of children. In the beginning, children may miss their breath when they pay attention to the vowel. It requires total concentration. It improves the concentration power of the kids.

Phase II

Way

I step – exhale out

II step – inhale in

III step – Laugh in silence

IV step – Relax at least 6 breaths, and then restart the next vowel.

Phase III

Way It is to remind of the two phases of laughter only within the mind, sitting in meditative posture and thinking how you have laughed in the two earlier phases.

Laughing with Clapping

Our palms are used for clapping. When we clap, all the points of all the organs, glands and tissues clash against each other and as a result, all the glands get activated.

The beating the palms against each other spurts the flow of life current profusely necessary to maintain good health, because according to acupressure therapy, rubbing and clapping the palms is very important from the healing point of view.

Laughter and clapping is very effective to heal the mind and body. That is why, when some one is happy, he not only laughs but also claps. The laughter and clapping energizes each and every nerve and cell of the body. In this way, the whole body gets stamina and maintains immunity. So laugh and clap. Be happy and healthy.

Benefits of Hasayam

Through Hasayam, all three problems–physical, mental and spiritual –are deleted from the screen of life. Trials and tribulations are reduced for the practitioner.

The river Ganga has been flowing from time immemorial and through dams and barrages, the flow of water is stopped and used to generate electricity or power. This power is used to build the nation. In the same way, if the natural process of laughing is stopped and the stopped breath is used to laugh in a particular tone –A.I.U.E.O. AM etc–then the generated energy heals each and every cell and nerve of the body. Laughter generated energy gives a lot of benefits at physical, mental and spiritual levels.

Physical Benefits

While laughing the belly vibrates, which is very healing. It stimulates the navel portion where all the glands –the prostate, Cowper's and adrenal glands get energy. The pancreas and islet of Langerhans also get activated which is responsible for insulin secretion and insulin harmone controls sugar in the body. Proper activation of the glands gets acute protection from diabetes, heart problem, prostate problems, kideny problem. The adrenal gland maintains all the metabolic functions. The proper functioning of adrenal gland promots harmonal secretion from pituitary glands, because meditative posture prepares ground for secretion of the glands.

The root cause of diabetes is tension. Continuous tension stops the functioning of the pituitary gland, a master gland. When this gland does not secrete the harmones for the proper functioning of so many glands within the body, not only diabetes but several other diseases occur.

So Laughter is a totaly remedy and preventive cure. It is exercised while sitting in a meditative posture. Meditative posture is prescribed for laughter.

The Hasayam is an advanced Pranayam. The benefits of Pranayam are gained by laughter. When adrenal gland acts properly, spleen also acts properly, and there can be no scope for cancer or blood cancer.

Yogic exercises should not be practised after meals but Hasayam or laughter can be practised after meals. After meals, it digests the food properly. Through regular practice of laughter therapy, there can be no obesity, no acidity, no gastric trouble. No diabetes, no migrane etc. Regular practitioner of laughter makes one free of ailments.

Psychological Benefits

When the quantum of lactate increases in the body, then impatience, nervousness take place in the nature of a person. The person feels uneasiness, unquiet. At this mental stress, laughter works as a psycho-therapy when sitting in a meditative posture. It has to be practised immediately. Then the quantity of lactate is minimized and as a result the person feels patient, easy, quiet. The practitioner feels happy, energetic and enthusiastic.

When anyone enjoys laughing, it means there is no depression in him. Laughing is a natural way to make a man happy, full of zeal, full of confidence, full of love and sympathy for all beings. Laughter generates energy. It activates the mystic points or Chakras, which give the practitioner perpetual peace. Laughter protects from depression, dementia, stress and distress, irritation and frustration. If any one practises it once in the morning, he feels happiness. Laughter provides the stamina and capacity to face the depressive situations in daily life.

Spiritual Benefits

Third phase of laughter is nothing but a state of meditation. All the benefits of meditation are the benefits of laughter also.

All the benefits of meditation can be considered as spiritual benefit of Hasayam.

The third phase is a meditative state because in the first phase, loud laughing is done and one by one in all the vowels, A.I.U.E.O. AM etc. In the second phase silent laughing is done. Both the phases provide a great deal of relaxation and a state of tranquility. In such a tranquil state of mind, the pituitary gland becomes activated and secretes many hormones. This hormonal secretion is the secret to good health of body, mind and the spirit. This gland and its secretions are responsible for all the metabolic functions within the body. Laughter is a complete therapy. This is a complete preventive therapy and a complete protective therapy.

Scientists have not yet examined how the hormones are acquired. Why not through self realization? I hope in the near future it will be proved that laughter is not a laughing matter. It is, seriously, a way to good health and of self realization.

ॐ ॐ ॐ

Eight
Cow and Kids

"Killing a bull is equivalent to killing a cow."

— **Jesus Christ**

"Cow's milk is tonic. It's ghee is ambrosia and it's meat is disease."

— **Hazarat Mohammad**

"Cow is source of progress and prosperity. In many ways, it is superior to one's mother."

— **Mahatma Gandhi**

Cow and Kids

Cows and children are complement to each other. Without cows, children cannot get proper nutrition. Now a days, children are victims of malnutrition and ill health, because of unavailability of cow milk and cow ghee in sufficient quantity.

If a child gets cow milk and butter during teenage, he/she can never be the victim of malnutrition or ill health. The brain of the child will be very sharp and prolific. The child will be intelligent, decent and efficient and scholarly, and grow as a man/woman of vim and vigour.

Lord Krishna, who was God himself, used to eat butter and roti for morning breakfast. In ancient times, cows and cow products – milk, ghee, curd, butter – were available in plenty. There was no dearth of milk or ghee.

The place where ten thousand cows lived was called Gokul. The person who kept five million cows was called Upanand. The person who reared nine million of cows was called Nand. The person who reared ten million cows was called Vrishbhanu and the person who rearerd fifty million cows was called Vrishbhanuver. The one who reared one million, a thousand to a hundred cows was called Gopal. In the Mahabharata it is mentioned that the Pandvas had eight

million sections of cows, and in each section there were a hundred cows, in this way eight crore cows were in the Pandva Goshala or cowsheds.

In Vedic scriptures, the cow has been declared as a nonkillable 'aghnya'. In ancient times, all Indians took milk and offered milk and butter milk, chhach to guests. It was said, one who drinks 'takram' or butter milk after lunch or breakfast, never goes to the doctor.

Lord Krishna was a cowherd according to scriptures. In Indian culture three mothers are considered (1) The mother who gives birth. (2) The cow who gives nourishment, nutrition, health and stamina. (3) Mother Earth who gives her lap to everyone at life's end. We have to respect all the mothers and should be greatful to them always.

Utility of the Cow

The cow is very useful for children, even the presence of a cow is said to be very healing and salubrious, because of her electromagnetic effect. When one touches a cow and rubs his/her palm over her body, then one comes under the influence of the electromagnetic field of the cow. The electric waves and the magnetic waves give a positive, healing and hygienic vibration, a boost to immunity and resistance against the contagious diseases.

Utility of Milk for Kids

Cow's milk is necter for children. It is easily digestible and goes to each and every nerve of the brain and body. To sharpen the mind and to lighten the body, cow's milk is very necessary. Nothing can substitute for cow milk for children. According to Bhav Prakash Nighantu, cow's milk contains tonic, energy and is conducive to heart and brain, increasing age and longevity. It maintains power and potency, resistance and immunity. Three defects in traditional ayurveda, Vat, Pitta and Kaf, are controlled with cow milk.

According to cardiologist Shantilal Shah, cow's milk is not harmful for a

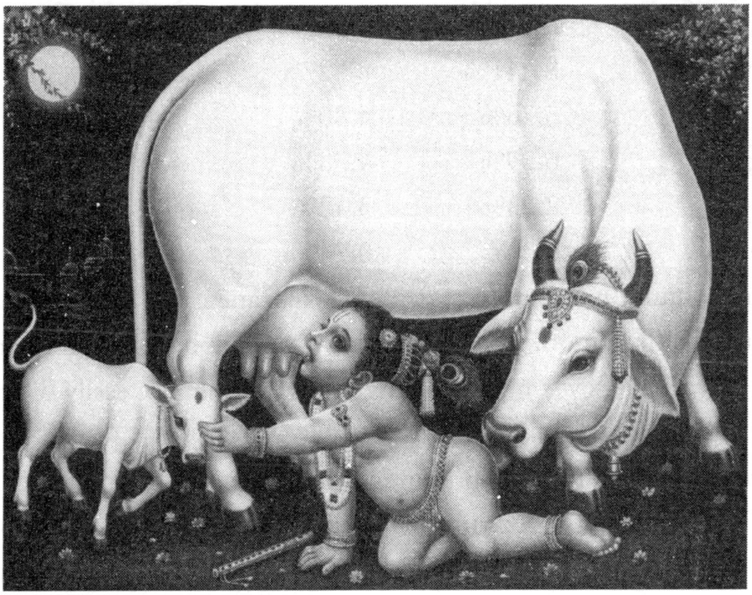

heart patient because it does not increase the cholesterol within the body. Cow's milk contains a yellow substance called Keratin (Vitamin A) which strengthens eye sight.Cow's milk contains ten times more keratin than buffalo milk.

Cow' milk is a complete food.Cow milk is rich in all known vitamins. Milk in fact is the only single article of food that fairly represents a complete diet. Milk is the best nutrition option for promotion and growth of kids, doctors say. A newspaper survey has recently said, IQ of the children who drink cow milk is very good.

Large quantities of benign microbes are found in cow milk, curd and butter milk (chhach). There is sufficient gold found in cow milk, which is said to act as antidote and antibody. Cow milk contains friendly microbes which protect from verious diseases.

Cow's milk has all the qualities of mother's milk. The Chart given below compares the milk of mother, cow and buffalo.

Materials	Mother	Cow	Buffalo
Water	87.41%	87.27%	82.14%
Fat	3.76%	4.80%	7.44%
Sugar	6.29%	4.78%	4.81%
Protine	2.23%	3.42%	4.78%
Minerals	0.3%	0.73%	0.83%

Calcium, sodium, potasium, copper, zinc, maganese and other minerals are found in the milk of mother and buffalo but-iron, sulphur and iodine are found only in cow milk. Cow's milk contains lactose and is very easily digestible. It provides agility and enthusiasm.

Cow milk is said to be helpful in increasing the height of children, as well as eye sight. Children who drink cow milk since childhood and up to the age 25, will not have to use glasses. The chart given below compares the height of children who drink milk and those who do not.

	Milk drinker kids		Non- drinker kids	
5 years	1.5	inch	1.2	inch
6 years	1.4	inch	1.1	inch
7 years	1.3	inch	1.2	inch
8 years	1.1	inch	1.2	inch
9 years	1.6	inch	1.1	inch

Today's children will be tomorrow's responsible citizens, how will they grow if they do not get cow milk to drink?

Utility of Ghee for Children

Cow's butter and butter oil (Ghee) is very beneficial for children. Cow butter gives good resistance and immunity to kids. It advances the beauty and charm of the body and face. It increases glow and shine of the skin and personality. It is a blood purifier. It protects from paralysis and asthma. Cow's Ghee is helpful for eye sight. It improves digestion, it is a brain tonic. It gives long life to children.

Scientists and doctors say that cow ghee is to be used by heart patients, not any other fat or ghee. Cow ghee is said to have power to protect the human body from the ill effects of radioactive waves. Just10 gms of cow ghee used in fire sacrifice produces one ton of oxygen. Sacrifice done with ghee purifies the environment and induces rain. In India, the fire sacrifice or Yagna is a tradition. **Note** Here cow means the original, Indian or indigenous breed, not hybrid cattle.

Utility of Cow Urine and Dung

Cow urine is said to contains copper which transforms into gold in the human body. Gold has the power to destroy all disease germs and it is an antidote.

Besides copper, cow urine contains calcium, phosphorus, salts. carbonic acid, potash and lactose.

Cow urine contains 24 types of salts and medicines made from cow urine are used to cure several diseases.

Cow urine is a disinfectant and prophylactic and thus purifies the atmosphere and improves the fertility of land.

Fresh cow dung kills germs of malaria and tuberclosis.

Japan has used cow dung as protection from redioactivity.

It is the best of fertilizer and compost.

Japan has also made petrol from cow urine. The Kanpur Bhauti Goshala has made CNG from cow dung.

Cow urine, boiled with (neem) margo leaves, is an effective pesticide with no side effect.

According to a standard, per capita 15.30 ounce milk is required but in India, according to a recent census, there are only four cows per 100 people. How then can cow products be available in a sufficient quantity?

The only way to protect cows today is to promote cow rearing by youth. Rural youth need to be extended the required financial support and diary management courses to study. This will provide adequate amount of cow milk for today's children.

How to Prepare Kajal (soot)

Plain soot (Kajal)

Powder of burnt, cow ghee, is called Kajal. This means a wick is dipped in ghee and burnt and the wick emits carbon. This carbon or soot is collected on a metal plate smeared with ghee.

Quantity 10 grams powder 1gm ghee or as required, to make it smoother.

Note Take all the remnants of the wick on a pineapple leaf or a clay pot, copper pot or brass pot.

Herbal soot (Kajal)

Way The process of it is the same but four herbs are also to be added. These are

1. Turmeric (haldi)
2. Betelnut(Supari)
3. Myrobalan(harad)
4. Thyme (Ajwain)

Quantity One gram each into 10 gms of wick powder.

Note Soak all the four herbs in cow ghee, and when the ghee gets absorbed fully, then add back the powder of these herbs into the powder to smear.

ॐ ॐ ॐ